LEAD WITH
PURPOSE

or don't bother

AN ANTI-GUIDE TO
INTENTIONAL LEADERSHIP

BRANDY PURCELL

ELECTRIC
MOON
PUBLISHING

Electric Moon Publishing & Media, LLC
PO Box 96
Bonner Springs, KS 66012
info@emoonpublishing.com

Editing by Jessie Steffes
Cover and Interior Design by Lyn Rayn / Electric Moon Publishing Creative Services
Printed in the United States of America

ELECTRIC
MOON
PUBLISHING

www.emoonpublishing.com

CONTENTS

INTRODUCTION

Hi, my name is Brandy

I've spent nearly twenty years helping organizations get their act together, from cleaning up messy processes to breathing life back into teams and cultures that forgot what "human" feels like.

These days, I help drive organizational effectiveness strategy in the wonderfully complex (and occasionally absurd) world of fintech banking, where change moves faster than compliance can draft a policy, and "business as usual" is a phrase we retired years ago. It's a space that keeps you humble, caffeinated, and perpetually updating your to-do list.

I'm also wrapping up a PhD in Industrial and Organizational Psychology because apparently, I'm committed to studying human behavior *and* living it in real time.

The reality is that no degree, title, or alphabet soup after your name magically fixes anything. Real change comes from the unglamorous stuff; showing up, making intentional choices, and doing the hard, human work that actually helps people and organizations thrive.

I care about this because I've seen what happens when workplaces start to *work* — when people are trusted, leaders lead with intention, and progress beats perfection. That's what this book is about.

No buzzwords. No ten-step frameworks. No "just manifest it" nonsense. Just honest, practical ideas (with a dash of humor) to help you lead better, starting right where you are.

Let's dive in.

Welcome to

THE ANTI-GUIDE

L et's get one thing straight: this isn't another leadership book written by someone who thinks they've cracked the code on human behavior or how to "inspire your people."

If you're looking for tidy frameworks, buzzwords, or a list of "10 proven steps to build trust in 30 days," you're in the wrong place. Those belong in the corporate landfill next to unused mission statements and half-finished engagement surveys.

This book is for people who actually care — who want to build workplaces where humans don't just survive the week but genuinely want to show up, contribute, and grow. It's for leaders (and future leaders) who are tired of the noise, allergic to bureaucracy, and ready to rethink what leadership really looks like.

The first half of this book will challenge how you think about leadership: the mindsets, assumptions, and good intentions that might be quietly sabotaging your culture. The second half will challenge how you do leadership: the daily actions that transform good ideas into meaningful change.

You'll find stories, research, and a few uncomfortable truths. You'll also find humor, because if we can't laugh at the absurdity of corporate life, we'll never survive it.

There are no perfect answers here, just better questions — and a whole lot of ways to lead with intention.

Take a deep breath. Ditch the jargon. Let's rebuild leadership from the roots up, one conversation, one team, one choice at a time.

BURN THE PLAYBOOK

(Manifesto)

Most organizations aren't broken in loud, headline-grabbing ways. They fray quietly — one skipped check-in, one "we'll circle back," one "urgent" deck — until the work leaves people running on fumes — disconnected from why they started.

This is your anti-guide. Not because rebellion is trendy, but because you don't need another one-size-fits-all framework. You need something that brings you back to what matters.

You won't find radical new theories here. Much of this will feel like common sense — because it is. But in the whirlwind of deadlines and meetings that should've been emails, we forget. We lose sight of what good leadership looks like: caring deeply, showing up consistently, and doing the simple, hard things with intention.

Think of this as a reset. A reminder manual. A book about

noticing again. Caring again. Choosing people, on purpose, again.

If you've ever:

- Canceled a 1:1 (again) because your calendar is stacked
- Promised to follow up with a struggling teammate... and didn't
- Spent more time polishing slides than talking to your team
- Skipped lunch, breaks, and breathing because everything felt "urgent"
- Realized you haven't said a genuine thank-you in weeks—not from apathy, but exhaustion

...this book is for you.

We're not here to put lipstick on broken systems or pretend a new mission statement will fix a trust problem. We're here to lead like humans and prove that meaningful work isn't a myth.

A Quick Reality Check

Too many organizations still operate like it's 1995: top-down memos, output worship, process over people. It's not just outdated; it's harmful.

To cope, we tell ourselves believable stories:

- "I'd love to check in with the team, but I'm too busy right now."
- "We'll address culture after this next project."
- "It's not ideal, but it's working well enough for now."
- "I don't have time to rethink how we do everything."

Those thoughts feel reasonable in the moment. Stacked day after day, they become the culture. The way things are. Eventually the organization stops thriving on energy and starts surviving on burnout.

Organizations don't change. People do. If you're reading this, you're probably one of them.

This isn't about theory. It's about reminders, reframing, and refocusing. Real work, done day by day, person by person, moment by moment.

Think Differently:
The Shift

- Question what feels "normal."
- Prioritize trust over rules.
- Choose progress over perfection, again and again.

Do Better:
The Invitation

No magic formulas. Something better: practical reflection, tiny shifts, real talk about the stuff we usually whisper.

We'll explore:

- What leadership actually means (spoiler: not titles)
- Why the obvious gets ignored, and how to fix it
- How small moves create outsized impact

One Last Thing
(Before We Dive In)

Reading won't change anything. Doing will.

Before you turn the page, name one thing that's broken in your world. Not the biggest, just the one that keeps nagging at you and is within your control. Commit to one concrete step this week. Not next quarter. Not after five meetings and a strategy deck. Start—on purpose.

Let's get to work.

Part One

THE MINDSET SHIFT

PEOPLE OVER PROFITS

(But Don't Forget the Profits)

Remember when Milton Friedman said a business's only responsibility is to make money? That thinking shaped decades of corporate culture — and it's long past its expiration date. The companies winning today aren't chasing profits; they're building legacies. They're human-centered, purpose-driven, and unafraid to challenge the idea that caring and success can't coexist.

Putting people first doesn't mean profits suffer, it means they *stick around.* When you take care of the people who make your business possible, they take care of the business.

The Power of Purpose

Some teams move with ease and energy while others can't seem to get out of first gear. That difference isn't luck, it's purpose. People-centered organizations look beyond short-term gains and create value that lasts.

~~~

- **The Shift:** Purpose isn't fluff — it's fuel.
  Example: Patagonia doesn't just sell outdoor gear; it sells conviction. Its mission to "save our home planet" shapes everything from product design to activism and earns fierce loyalty from customers and employees alike.
- **Why It Matters:** Purpose drives performance. When people know *why* their work matters, they care more and contribute better.

~~~

- **The Shift:** Mission statements don't mean a thing if they only live on a wall.
  Example: An architecture firm redefined its purpose from "clients first" to "people first," then made design choices that prioritized human well-being over cost savings. Clients noticed and lined up to work with them.
- **Why It Matters:** Authenticity isn't optional. People can tell when your purpose is performative.

Cheeky Tip

If your mission statement sounds like it was written by a committee after too much coffee, it probably was. Rewrite it in plain English — and mean it.

Why People Matter More Than Profits

Profits keep the lights on. People keep the lights bright. A thriving business recognizes that the heart of growth beats in its employees, customers, and community, not its spreadsheets.

~~~~~

- **The Shift:** Engagement is the ultimate ROI.
  Example: A tech startup with high turnover replaced micro-management with mentorship and recognition. Within a year, turnover dropped 25 percent and customer satisfaction skyrocketed.
- **Why It Matters:** When people feel seen and supported, they stay — and they lift everything around them.

~~~~~

- **The Shift:** Customers don't want products; they want connection.
  Example: A neighborhood coffee shop built loyalty by paying fair-trade prices and sponsoring local clean-ups. People didn't just buy coffee; they bought into a story that felt good to be part of.
- **Why It Matters:** Values attract loyalty. Authenticity builds community — and community builds profit.

~~~~~

- **The Shift:** Communities make brands believable.
  Example: A manufacturing company partnered with local schools for internships and STEM programs. The investment paid off with stronger community ties and a future talent pipeline.
- **Why It Matters:** Giving back isn't charity, it's smart business.

Cheeky Tip

If your "people-first" initiative involves a pizza party, congratulations — you've just invented the cheapest retention plan ever.

Breaking the Profit-First Mentality

The idea that people-centered leadership is "soft" is the corporate equivalent of a rotary phone — ancient, clunky, and irrelevant.

~~~~~

- **The Shift:** Measure what actually matters.
  Example: A global retailer added "employee-happiness scores" alongside revenue metrics. Fixing the people problems fixed the profit problems too.
- **Why It Matters:** You can't improve what you don't measure — and what you measure tells everyone what really matters.

~~~~~

- **The Shift:** Invest in development, not just output.
  Example: A mid-sized firm gave employees a "learning stipend" for courses of their choice. The company gained new ideas, energy, and retention — all for less than the cost of one bad hire.
- **Why It Matters:** Growth creates loyalty. People who feel invested in, invest back.

- **The Shift:** Pay fairly, period.
  Example: A startup tested a four-day workweek without cutting pay. Productivity rose, burnout plummeted, and everyone wondered why they hadn't done it sooner.
- **Why It Matters:** Fair pay and flexibility aren't perks — they're respect in action.

Cheeky Tip

If your exec team needs a luxury retreat to decide whether investing in people is worth it, skip to the part where you lose your best talent.

Living Your Values

Writing values is easy. Living them? That's leadership.

- **The Shift:** Transparency builds trust.
  Example: A CEO hosted monthly town halls to share both wins and challenges. Employees stopped speculating and started collaborating.
- **Why It Matters:** Openness invites ownership. When people understand what's happening, they engage with how to fix it.

~~~

- **The Shift**: Lead like a human, not a hero.
  Example: A COO publicly unplugged on vacation — and didn't answer emails. That single act modeled boundaries more effectively than any policy ever could.
- **Why It Matters:** People follow what you *do,* not what you say.

~~~

- **The Shift:** Gratitude fuels growth.
  Example: A company created a "Thank-You Wall" for peer shout-outs. The wall became a daily stop for dopamine and camaraderie.
- **Why It Matters:** Recognition doesn't just make people feel good — it makes them *do* good.

Cheeky Tip

If your office values are vinyl decals instead of daily habits, you've got expensive wallpaper, not culture.

Success Stories

- Patagonia: Turned activism into advantage — their purpose drives profits because people believe in it.
- The Coffee Collective: Scaled by connecting with community and making fair-trade part of their brand identity.
- Unnamed Financial Firm: Replaced bonuses with well-being benefits like childcare stipends and flexible hours. Turnover dropped 40 percent, and profits hit record highs.

Reflection Section

What's one policy, meeting, or metric in your organization that prioritizes profit over people?

What's one small shift you could make this month to reverse it?

Leader Lens

People-first leadership isn't soft; it's strategic. Model care and accountability in equal measure, and your team will mirror both.

Notes

Write down two or three small actions you can take this week to make your team feel genuinely valued.

Bringing It Together

Putting people first isn't a feel-good philosophy, it's a fearless strategy. It means trading quick wins for lasting impact and realizing that sustainable success doesn't come from squeezing more out of people but from giving them more to believe in.

Because here's the truth: profits don't disappear when you put people first — they deepen. They become more consistent, resilient, and meaningful. The best organizations aren't just productive; they're *alive* — humming with purpose and shared meaning.

A business that grows at the expense of its people isn't growing at all. The ones that endure are led by those who see the connection between care and performance — and have the courage to lead from that place, even when it's not convenient.

✩ *Your Challenge* ✩

This week, make one decision with your people in mind first — not your budget, not your board. Your *people*. You'll be surprised how often the profits follow.

Cheeky Reminder:
"Business isn't personal"? Please. It's *all* personal.

(2)

SHARED VALUES AND MISSION
*More Than
Just Words*

You've seen it before: a shiny mission statement plastered across office walls, slide decks, and onboarding packets. Words like *Integrity*, *Innovation*, and *Teamwork* carefully chosen in a two-hour meeting — followed by a group high-five and a long nap. Then…crickets.

The "values" gather dust while everyone goes back to business as usual.

Values and mission statements aren't decoration; they're direction. They're meant to guide behavior, fuel purpose, and align people toward something that actually matters. And when they're co-created with the people who live them, not dictated by a leadership echo chamber — they become more than words. They become movement.

Why Shared Values and Mission Matter

A mission isn't about sounding profound; it's about creating clarity. Values aren't about slogans; they're about standards. Together, they tell your people why they're here and how to show up.

~~~~~

- **The Shift:** Values shape behavior long before policies do.
  Example: A company claims to prize "collaboration" but only rewards individual wins. The result? Competition disguised as culture.
- **Why It Matters:** When your incentives fight your values, your people stop believing both.

~~~~~

- **The Shift:** Success is more than metrics, it's how you achieve them.
  Example: A sales rep who helps teammates close deals may sell less personally but drives more collective revenue. Recognize that person, or risk losing them.
- **Why It Matters:** If you only celebrate outcomes, you'll get results without relationships, and burnout for dessert.

~~~~~

- **The Shift:** Mission gives people a reason to care.
  Example: Patagonia's promise to "save our home planet" isn't a tagline; it's a compass guiding daily decisions, from sourcing fabric to volunteering hours.
- **Why It Matters:** When the mission feels real, people act like it is.

Cheeky Tip

If your mission is "To be the leading provider of [insert product here]," congratulations — you've written the corporate equivalent of elevator music. Inspire, don't tranquilize.

How to Make Values and Mission Real

- **The Shift:** Involve your people from the start.
  Example: A tech startup ran a company-wide workshop asking, "What do we stand for?" The resulting values were messy, honest, and completely theirs.
- **Why It Matters:** People commit to what they help create. Top-down values rarely reach ground level.

- **The Shift:** Embed your values into every decision.
  Example: During interviews, one company asks candidates, "Tell me about a time you collaborated with someone difficult." They're not testing skill — they're testing alignment.
- **Why It Matters:** Hiring for values protects culture faster than any handbook can.

- **The Shift:** Model the message.
  Example: A CEO who invites open debate and admits mistakes demonstrates humility and curiosity — two words you can't fake on a poster.

- **Why It Matters:** Culture is what leaders tolerate, celebrate, and imitate.

> ## Cheeky Insight ✍
> If your exec team preaches "transparency" but operates like a secret society, your employees have already created the meme.

When Values and Mission Go Wrong

- **The Shift:** Misalignment kills trust faster than mistakes.
  Example: A company touts "work-life balance" while sending 11 p.m. emails. No one believes the slogan anymore.
- **Why It Matters:** Hypocrisy is the ultimate disengagement strategy.

~~~~

- **The Shift:** Consistency beats complexity.
  Example: A company declares 14 values — no one remembers even three. The list becomes a trivia question, not a guide.
- **Why It Matters:** Fewer values, lived loudly, beat long lists recited rarely.

> ## Cheeky Tip ✍
> If employees have to Google your values before reciting them, start over.

Success Stories:
Values and Mission in Action

- ⬥ **Southwest Airlines:** "To connect people to what's important in their lives." Every employee, from pilot to gate agent, owns kindness as part of the job description.
- ⬥ **Zappos:** "Deliver WOW Through Service." They once spent eight hours on the phone helping one customer find the perfect pair of shoes. Legendary.
- ⬥ **The Container Store:** "Organize Lives." Their "1 equals 3" philosophy — that one great employee equals the output of three average ones — drives hiring and development.
- ⬥ **Micro-Case Study: The Mission Makeover**
At a midsize nonprofit, no one could recite the mission, it was corporate oatmeal. Leadership hosted workshops to rewrite it in plain language rooted in daily work. The new statement was short, human, and inspiring. Within 18 months, engagement scores jumped and fundraising doubled. Turns out clarity pays.

Reflection Section

If you asked five employees to describe your mission and values, would their answers match yours, or even each other's?

Leader Lens

Leaders don't just communicate values; they translate them into action. Every decision is a broadcast of what you truly believe. Make sure your actions aren't running ads for a brand you don't represent.

Notes

Sketch the values you wish your team lived by. How different are they from what's written on paper?

What's one behavior that could start closing that gap this week?

Bringing It Together

Shared values and mission aren't corporate accessories, they're your organization's DNA. They shape who you attract, how you act, and whether people feel proud to wear your logo on their hoodie or secretly browse LinkedIn at lunch.

The best companies don't treat values as wallpaper; they treat them as a way of life. When you embed meaning into every decision, people stop showing up for a paycheck and start showing up with purpose. That's when momentum builds. That's when culture becomes contagious.

Your values are only as believable as your worst behavior. If leaders preach "respect" but play favorites, or say "innovation" while punishing mistakes, the message is clear, and it's not the one on your website.

Real values live in micro-moments: the decisions made under pressure, the conversations you don't prepare for, the emails sent after a hard day. That's where culture is born — and where mission either thrives or dies.

✦ *Your Challenge* ✦

Pick one company value and audit it this week. Is it real? Is it lived? If not, don't rewrite the words, rewrite the behavior.

Cheeky Reminder:
If your values wouldn't survive a bad Monday,
they aren't values—they're marketing.

(3)

REDEFINING CULTURE

It's the Little Things

Culture isn't free snacks, quirky job titles, or a Slack emoji explosion. It's how people feel when they show up — whether that's in an office, at home, or on a call while balancing coffee, chaos, and carpool.

A thriving culture isn't built overnight or through gimmicks. It's shaped by the quiet, everyday details that define how people interact, collaborate, and grow together. In short: culture lives in the moments you're not trying to "build" it.

What Culture Isn't

Let's start with what it's *not*.

~~~

- **The Shift:** Perks are temporary; culture is permanent. *Example:* Picture an office overflowing with perks — catered lunches, ping-pong tables, kombucha on tap — but no psychological safety. Sure, people enjoy the free snacks, but no one feels safe speaking up.
- **Why It Matters:** Perks can't fix fear. When safety's missing, no amount of yoga rooms or company swag will make up for it.

~~~

- **The Shift:** Policies don't define culture, people do. *Example:* A company proudly advertises a "flexible work" policy, but managers still expect instant replies at 10 p.m. That's not flexibility; that's burnout in disguise.
- **Why It Matters:** Culture is what people experience, not what leaders announce.

Cheeky Insight

If your culture needs a PowerPoint to be understood, it's probably not being felt.

How to Build a Thriving Culture

- **The Shift:** Watch your language.
  Example: Stop calling people "resources." They're humans, not supply chain items. Even small shifts — "team" instead of "staff," "people" instead of "headcount" — change tone and connection.
- **Why It Matters:** Language reflects values. Every word either builds belonging or builds walls.

〰️

- **The Shift:** Recognition is the heartbeat of belonging.
  Example: One company launched a "Kudos Corner" where employees highlighted peers' efforts — from closing big deals to surviving brutal deadlines. Soon, meetings started with gratitude instead of grumbling.
- **Why It Matters:** Recognition, done right, doesn't just celebrate, it energizes.

〰️

- **The Shift:** Design spaces people actually want to be in.
  Example: A company turned a dusty conference room into a "Recharge Zone" — comfy chairs, plants, and no laptops allowed. Morale lifted, creativity followed. For remote teams, a weekly "no-meeting hour" had the same effect.
- **Why It Matters:** The space you give people — physical or mental — says more about your values than your mission statement ever will.

- **The Shift:** Build relationships that outlast deadlines.
  Example: A hybrid company introduced casual "coffee chats" between random colleagues across departments. People found common ground, shared ideas, and even solved problems that had nothing to do with their titles.
- **Why It Matters:** Connection fuels collaboration. People work harder and smarter when they actually like each other.

Cheeky Tip

If your only "team-building" involves mandatory trust falls, congratulations — you've built resentment, not culture.

Culture Is in the Details

A great culture isn't about grand gestures. It's about the quiet consistency of care. It shows up in how leaders listen, how decisions are made, and how values are lived when no one's watching.

- **The Shift:** Accountability builds authenticity.
  Example: One company tied executive bonuses to employee engagement scores. Suddenly, leaders started asking better questions — and actually listening to the answers.
- **Why It Matters:** What gets measured gets prioritized. When leadership is accountable for culture, everyone takes it seriously.

> ## Cheeky Insight
>
> If your culture can't survive a bad day or a blunt email, it wasn't that strong to begin with.

Micro-Case Study:
Culture Isn't a Couch

A startup once spent thousands on beanbags, neon signs, and endless LaCroix — but skipped basic respect. Employee feedback revealed toxic communication and zero trust. The CEO scrapped the perks and trained managers on psychological safety. One year later, productivity rose 22%, and Glassdoor reviews finally matched the job posts.

Turns out, culture doesn't need couches — it needs care.

Reflection Section

Think about the last time someone felt included — or excluded — at work. What unspoken norms or habits allowed that to happen?

Leader Lens

Culture is built in micro-moments. Every "thank you," every tone in an email, every time you listen instead of interrupt — it all stacks up.

As a leader, your daily habits shape the climate more than any all-hands speech ever could.

Notes

List a few small ways you could reinforce the culture you *say* you want to build:

▶ One thing you'll do today

▶ One thing you'll do this month

▶ One thing you'll make a habit

Wrapping It Up

Culture isn't the loudest thing in your company, it's the most constant. It lives in how people treat each other on an average Tuesday, how feedback is given after mistakes, and how safe it feels to be honest.

Forget the slogans and the perks. The real markers of culture are invisible but unmistakable:

- Safety that's felt, not promised
- Belonging that doesn't depend on title
- Leaders who model humanity over hierarchy

If you want to know your true culture, listen for it. It's in the pauses, the laughter, the honesty — those quiet "I've got you" moments that never make a report.

That's the heartbeat of a healthy organization.

Your Challenge

Pay attention this week. Notice the small things — the language, the tone, the follow-through. That's your culture talking. If you don't like what it's saying, start rewriting the script.

Cheeky Reminder:
You can't *build* culture.
You can only *live* it.

THE ENVIRONMENT MATTERS

And It's Not Just About Offices

Let's talk about *where* you work.

Not the company name on your badge or the logo glowing from your laptop — the actual space where you think, create, and occasionally question your life choices over a reheated cup of coffee.

Whether it's your kitchen table, a coworking lounge, or an open-plan office with the acoustics of a food court, your environment matters — a lot.

Where you work shapes how you work. It influences your mood, your energy, and whether you leave the day inspired or emotionally drained.

And the real kicker? Your environment — physical *and* digital — is always talking. It tells people what you value, what you ignore, and how much you actually care.

If your setup makes you dread Mondays, that's not laziness,

that's a design failure. And if your "wellness room" doubles as a supply closet? Time for an intervention.

Why Environment Matters

- **The Reality Check:** Space shapes behavior.
  Example: An ad agency swapped beige walls for murals by local artists. Suddenly, brainstorms stopped sounding like group therapy and started sparking actual ideas.
- **Why It Matters:** Creativity doesn't bloom in beige. Intentional environments cue imagination, and remind people they're not robots.

- **The Takeaway:** Your surroundings affect mental health more than you think.
  Example: A nonprofit traded its fluorescent cave for natural light, ergonomic seating, and quiet pods. Stress dropped. Engagement soared. Migraines became myths.
- **Why It Matters:** People can't do great work when their backs hurt and their brains are fried. Physical comfort drives emotional well-being.

- **The Wake-Up Call:** Your space tells the truth about your values.
  Example: A sustainability-focused company used reclaimed wood, solar panels, and walls of greenery. It wasn't about Instagram — it was alignment in action.
- **Why It Matters:** Environments are statements. The only question is whether yours is intentional or accidental.

Cheeky Insight

If your lighting makes everyone look like they're in a crime documentary, don't expect bright ideas.

Designing Environments That Work

- **The Pivot:** Design for different kinds of work.
  Example: One firm created zones — quiet for focus, collaborative for brainstorming, open for connection. Meetings got shorter, noise complaints disappeared, and headphones were optional again.
- **Why It Matters:** People have different rhythms. Great space flexes with them instead of forcing adaptation to bad architecture.

- **The Move:** Comfort is productivity.
  Example: Adjustable desks, decent chairs, and coffee that doesn't taste like punishment. These aren't perks — they're physical respect.
- **Why It Matters:** Innovation dies when your spine's in revolt.

- **The Upgrade:** Let people personalize their space.
  Example: A "Pimp My Desk" challenge gave employees permission to decorate. The result? A floor full of creativity, ownership, and plants with names.

- **Why It Matters:** Ownership fuels pride. When people see themselves in their space, they show up differently.

~~~

- **The Energy Shift:** Energy beats efficiency.
  Example: A coworking hub added a rooftop garden. Meetings moved outdoors, ideas flowed, and no one missed the fluorescent buzz.
- **Why It Matters:** People aren't batteries to be drained; they're engines to be fueled.

Cheeky Tip

If your "collaboration area" is just one sad table, a dry-erase marker, and a dying fern, congratulations — you've built a shrine to mediocrity.

Where Companies Get It Wrong

- **The Lesson:** Basics before aesthetics.
  Example: One office installed a slide between floors before fixing the broken HVAC. Guess what employees cared about when July hit?
- **Why It Matters:** Broken basics break morale. You can't design your way out of dysfunction.

~~~

- **The Principle:** Accessibility is culture, not compliance.
  Example: A company redesigned its HQ with adjustable desks, inclusive sound zones, and clear navigation paths.

Morale rose — and so did legal peace of mind.

- **Why It Matters:** If your space excludes even one person, it's not innovative; it's incomplete.

〜〜〜

- **The Reminder:** Instagram isn't your audience.
  Example: That office slide might rack up likes, but if no one uses it (or sprains an ankle on it), it's not a culture win.
- **Why It Matters:** People want usable spaces, not photo ops.

> ## Cheeky Tip
> If your team spends more time posting about your office than working in it, that's décor — not design.

When It Works:
Real-World Examples

- ◇ **Airbnb:** Their meeting rooms are modeled after actual listings — cabins, lofts, beach houses. The space *feels* like the mission: belonging anywhere.
- ◇ **Pixar:** Their central atrium was built to force collisions — creative ones. Unplanned encounters fuel cross-pollination.
- ◇ **Startup Success:** After ditching a windowless cave for a light-filled, plant-packed loft, productivity jumped 20%. No one missed the old Keurig.

Micro-Case Study:
From Cubicles to Connection

After going remote, a mid-sized tech company watched its culture fade. HR launched "Digital Campfires" — casual, no-agenda video meetups. They became lifelines. One employee joked, "I haven't seen Bob's legs in two years, but I feel closer to him than ever."

- **Why It Matters:** Connection doesn't depend on proximity. It depends on presence.

Reflection Section

What story does your workspace — physical or digital — tell about your team?

Does it reflect who you *are* or who you *used to be*?

Leader Lens

Environment is quiet leadership. It either builds energy or drains it.

You're responsible for curating the spaces — digital and physical — where your people think, connect, and recharge. Not just for paying the lease.

Notes

Describe your current workspace in three words.

Now describe the one you *want*.

What would need to change to close the gap?

Wrapping It Up

Your environment speaks even when you don't. Every wall, chair, and Slack channel sends a message about what you value and how much you care.

A great environment doesn't just look good, it *feels* good. It helps people think clearly, breathe easier, and bring their best ideas to life. It quietly whispers, *"You matter here."*

Take a lap — literally or mentally — around your workspace. What's it saying? Is it fueling creativity, focus, and belonging? Or quietly muttering, *"meh"*?

You don't need nap pods or neon signs, you need intention. Thoughtful design is empathy in physical form. When people feel supported by their environment, everything else — trust, collaboration, performance — follows naturally.

✴ *Your Challenge* ✴

Pick one small environmental change this week that will make your people's day 1% better. Then actually do it.

$$\left(5\right)$$

LEADERSHIP

Not a Title,
Not a Threat,
Always Earned

Leadership isn't about wielding authority, it's about earning trust.

It's not about titles, corner offices, or how many people report to you. It's how you show up, how you treat people, and how you inspire them to act — not because they *have to*, but because they *want to*.

But let's be real: titles can make even the nicest leader intimidating. That "power aura" can freeze a room faster than bad Wi-Fi. When that happens, great ideas stay unspoken, creativity flatlines, and your culture quietly shifts from brave to cautious.

True leadership is never demanded, it's demonstrated. It's not what your title gives you; it's what your team grants you.

When Power Warps the Room

- **Reality Check:** Power changes the room, even when you don't mean it to.
  Example: The CEO walks into a meeting, says nothing, and starts typing furiously. The team stops breathing. Are they mad? Bored? Plotting world domination? No one knows — so everyone plays it safe.
- **Why It Matters:** Silence can be scarier than shouting. If people are guessing what you think instead of telling you what *they* think, your culture's in trouble.

~~~

- **Observation:** Titles amplify everything.
  Example: A well-meaning "Chief Something" can accidentally send *Proceed with Caution* vibes without saying a word. It's not intent — it's perception.
- **Why It Matters:** Influence without accessibility breeds fear, not respect.

Cheeky Insight

If your team goes quiet the moment you walk in, congratulations — you're a human mute button.

The Profit-Over-People Problem

Let's name the elephant in the boardroom: fear-based leadership works — for a while. It hits quarterly goals, checks compliance boxes, and keeps everyone "in line."

But it also breeds burnout, turnover, and a culture where people do just enough to stay out of trouble.

- **The Wake-Up Call:** Fear gets results; trust gets repeat results.
  Example: One VP ruled by intimidation — and their team hit every number but lost half its people within a year. Their replacement led with clarity, gratitude, and owner-ship. Same metrics, zero attrition.
- **Why It Matters:** People don't leave companies; they leave fear.

- **The Reminder:** Approachability and profitability aren't opposites.
  Example: A leader who listens before deciding gets better data, faster innovation, and fewer fires to put out.
- **Why It Matters:** Trust costs nothing — and pays in loyalty, creativity, and speed.

Cheeky Tip
If your leadership style only works when people are afraid of you, that's not leadership — that's a hostage situation.

What Great Leaders Actually Do

- **The Constant:** Leadership sets the tone — always.
  Example: A director who shares context and decisions openly builds trust. One who hoards information builds rumors.
- **Why It Matters:** Transparency scales faster than secrecy.

~~~~~

- **The Move:** Trust isn't a speech; it's a series of small choices.
  Example: A manager who says, "Here's where I dropped the ball — and how I'll fix it," models accountability. One who says, "Who messed this up?" models fear.
- **Why It Matters:** People trust what they *see*, not what they're told.

~~~~~

- **The Reality:** Inspiration beats intimidation.
  Example: A CEO paints a bold, inclusive vision — then connects it to each person's role. Suddenly, people aren't just clocking in; they're *bought in.*
- **Why It Matters:** Purpose fuels persistence.

~~~~~

- **The Shift:** Presence is power.
  Example: A leader who greets people by name, checks in genuinely, and remembers small details doesn't need a title to earn loyalty.
- **Why It Matters:** Leadership isn't loud — it's consistent.

The Bad and the Brilliant
The Terrible Leaders

- **Lesson One:** Control doesn't equal competence.
  Example: The micromanager who rewrites every email kills creativity faster than they can say "loop me in."
- **Why It Matters:** When leaders don't trust, teams stop trying.

~~~

- **Lesson Two:** Blame is the ultimate culture killer.
  Example: The "blame-shifter" who explodes publicly after a missed deadline teaches everyone one lesson: keep your head down.
- **Why It Matters:** People can't grow in defense mode.

~~~

- **Lesson Three:** Visibility means vulnerability.
  Example: The "invisible leader" vanishes in crisis but reappears for applause. Everyone sees it — and no one forgets it.
- **Why It Matters:** Leadership shows up most when things go sideways.

> **Cheeky Tip**
> The best thing about bad leaders?
> They make it painfully clear who
> you'll never be.

The Great Ones

- **Anchor Point:** Mentorship multiplies impact.
  Example: A senior director blocks time weekly to coach junior staff — and celebrates their wins more than their own.
- **Why It Matters:** Teaching is the most scalable form of leadership.

~~~

- **Principle:** Vision without ego.
  Example: A founder connects every team's work to a bigger *why,* not their own brand.
- **Why It Matters:** People don't follow arrogance, they follow authenticity.

~~~

- **Practice:** Listening *is* leadership.
  Example: A VP runs listening tours across departments, then actually acts on what they hear. Engagement spikes. Cynicism plummets.
- **Why It Matters:** Listening isn't passive — it's strategic awareness.

Cheeky Tip

If you've ever said, "I'd work for them again in a heartbeat," send that leader a thank-you note. Then become one yourself.

How to Be the Kind of Leader People Follow *(Not Fear)*

- **Guiding Move:** Lead by example.
  Example: Want balance? Don't send midnight emails. Want trust? Keep your word.
- **Why It Matters:** People don't do what you say — they mirror what you model.

~~~~~~

- **Mindset:** Transparency beats perfection.
  Example: "Here's what's hard, and here's how we're tackling it" builds confidence. "Everything's fine!" builds cynicism.
- **Why It Matters:** Vulnerability is credibility.

~~~~~~

- **Approach:** Autonomy isn't abdication — it's empowerment.
  Example: Set expectations, then step back. Micromanagement kills confidence faster than failure.
- **Why It Matters:** Ownership builds leaders, not followers.

~~~~~~

- **Habit:** Recognition is your superpower.
  Example: A public thank-you in a meeting or a handwritten note outperforms any motivational poster.
- **Why It Matters:** Appreciation compounds like interest.

~~~~~~

- **Long Game:** Invest in people, not just outcomes.
  Example: "You're not there yet — but here's how to get there" keeps doors open. "You're not what we're looking for" slams them shut.
- **Why It Matters:** Leaders build futures, not résumés.

Cheeky Insight

If your team's happiest day is when you're out of office, it's time for some soul-searching.

When Leadership Works:
Real-World Wins

- ◇ **Howard Schultz (Starbucks):** Built an empire on trust and inclusion. Calling baristas "partners" wasn't PR — it was strategy.
- ◇ **Jacinda Ardern (New Zealand):** Proved empathy and strength aren't opposites — they're a power couple.
- ◇ **The Everyday Leader:** A mid-level manager who hosted weekly "Ask Me Anything" sessions. Transparency soared. So did engagement.

Micro-Case Study:
The Unassuming Leader

When Maya was promoted, she skipped the "new sheriff" routine. She asked questions, admitted mistakes, and shared credit generously. Within three months, her team led the company in both performance and morale.

One teammate summed it up perfectly:

"She doesn't manage us. She leads with us."

- • **Why It Matters:** Real leadership isn't about authority — it's about alignment.

Reflection Section

Think of a time someone truly earned your trust. What made them credible, approachable, and real?

Leader Lens

Leadership is how you show up when no one's watching. It's earned through consistency, humility, and presence — not power, perfection, or PR.

Notes

List two habits that define your leadership style.

Are they building trust — or eroding it?

What would a courageous version of you change first?

Wrapping It Up

Leadership is a privilege, not a power trip. It's not about controlling people — it's about connecting with them and creating space for them to succeed, even in ways that make you less needed. That's the goal.

The best leaders don't hoard authority; they share it. They model calm in chaos, clarity in uncertainty, and compassion in conflict. They make hard choices without losing their humanity.

Think back to the leaders who've shaped your story — the good, the bad, and the unforgettable. What lessons did they leave behind? What kind of leader do you want your name to evoke?

Your Challenge

This week, lead like someone's watching — not your boss, but your team.

The goal isn't perfection; it's presence.

Cheeky Reminder:

If you're not lifting others up, you're not leading —
you're just managing.
And the world has enough managers.
Do better.

6

PSYCHOLOGICAL SAFETY

Why It Matters and How to Create it

L eadership isn't just about direction — it's about permission. Permission to speak. To question. To fail and try again.

You can have the clearest mission and the sharpest strategy, but if people don't feel safe to use their voices, none of it matters.

That's the quiet truth most leaders miss: innovation doesn't die from bad ideas — it dies from silence. The best cultures aren't built on perfection; they're built on *trust*, the kind that makes honesty possible and disagreement productive.

Before we talk about change management or communication plans, we have to start with something simpler and deeper: creating space where people don't just *show up*, but *show themselves.*

Psychological safety isn't a buzzword. It's the heartbeat of every high-performing team. Without it, meetings fill with polite nodding and quiet resentment. With it, people bring ideas, courage, and truth.

When people feel safe, you unlock creativity. When they don't, you get compliance and quiet exits.

So how do you build it?

Simple: don't terrify your team.

Why Psychological Safety Matters

Fear doesn't just stifle creativity — it rewires it into survival mode. Picture a team walking into a meeting buzzing with ideas, only for the boss to kick things off with, "Let's tear this apart." In seconds, the energy shifts from alive to polite. No one stops thinking; they just stop *sharing.* The fix isn't more positivity — it's curiosity. A leader who says, "Walk me through it," opens the door to better ideas. One who says, "That's not how we do it," slams it shut. Every time curiosity wins over judgment, innovation takes a step forward.

~~~

- **The Practice:** Vulnerability builds strength.
  Example: A manager admits, "I'm not sure what the best answer is here. Any thoughts?" The team leans in. Ideas multiply.
- **Why It Matters:** When leaders go first, everyone else feels safe to follow.

Cheeky Insight

If your team's best brainstorming happens *after* you leave the room, you've already found the problem.

How to Foster Psychological Safety

- **Perspective Shift:** Reward curiosity, not compliance.
  Example: A leader who says, "Interesting — tell me more," invites discovery. One who nods only when they agree trains people to play it safe.
- **Why It Matters:** Growth doesn't come from echo chambers. It comes from brave, messy conversations.

- **The Adjustment:** Feedback should feel like collaboration, not correction.
  Example: Replace "Who messed this up?" with "What can we do differently next time?"
- **Why It Matters:** People learn faster when feedback feels safe.

- **The Reminder:** Tone changes everything.
  Example: "Can you explain that?" can sound curious or condescending — same words, different tone.
- **Why It Matters:** Leaders set the emotional temperature of every conversation.

How to Wreck Psychological Safety
(and How to Fix It)

- **Red Flag:** Public shaming kills trust instantly.
  Example: "Who approved this? It's a disaster." In one sentence, you've taught everyone to stay quiet.
- **Why It Matters:** Humiliation sticks. People don't forget who made them small.

~~~~

- **Pattern to Break:** Ignoring feedback is leadership's quiet betrayal.
  Example: Someone offers an idea. You nod. Nothing happens. Next time? They don't bother.
- **Why It Matters:** If asking for input is performative, engagement evaporates.

~~~~

- **The Trap:** Blame is the fastest route to disengagement.
  Example: "Whose fault is this?" invites defensiveness. "What can we learn from this?" invites ownership.
- **Why It Matters:** Accountability builds growth; blame builds fear.

Rebuilding Safety (If You've Broken It)

- **The Reframe:** Focus on lessons, not losses.
  Example: "That campaign flopped, but here's what it taught us." That's not spin; it's forward motion.
- **Why It Matters:** People follow leaders who move forward, not ones who fixate on the wreckage.

~~~

- **The Restoration:** Transparency restores trust.
  Story: At a biotech company, employees quietly admitted to HR they were afraid to speak up — retaliation felt real. Instead of denial, leadership went all in: anonymous forums, open discussions, and visible changes. Within months, people stopped whispering and started contributing again.
- **Why It Matters:** Safety grows when words and actions finally match.

Cheeky Insight

Honesty isn't just saying what's true — it's proving people won't be punished for saying it too.

Real-World Inspiration:

Pixar's Braintrust

At Pixar, every film goes through "Braintrust" sessions where peers critique the work — no hierarchy, no ego, just shared purpose. The goal isn't to tear down a director; it's to make the story stronger.

- **The Lesson:** Feedback is a gift, not a grenade.
- **Why It Matters:** When feedback feels like support, creativity doesn't just improve — it soars.

Micro-Story:
The Meeting That Changed Everything

A mid-level manager named Luis once started every staff meeting with, "Any updates?" Cue the crickets.

One day, after a project tanked, he tried something different. He said, "Before we dive in — what did I miss as a leader that could've helped you succeed?"

The silence was heavy — then someone said, "Honestly? We didn't feel like we could tell you when things were off-track."

Luis didn't defend himself. He thanked them. A week later, he launched a new check-in: "What's working, what's weird, and what's worrying you?"

Within a month, performance rebounded. Not because he found the perfect strategy, but because he made it safe to tell the truth.

Reflection Section

Where in your organization do people hesitate to speak up?

What might they fear — embarrassment, rejection, or exhaustion?

Leader Lens

Psychological safety isn't about comfort; it's about courage.

It's not about lowering expectations — it's about removing fear so people can rise to meet them.

Notes

Would you share a risky idea in your current team?

If not, what would have to change — in you or in the environment — for that to feel safe?

Wrapping It Up

Psychological safety isn't fluff. It's the foundation of every culture that lasts.

It's not about coddling people — it's about trusting them enough to think out loud. Every reaction, every raised eyebrow, every sigh communicates safety or threat. When leaders create safety, teams bring truth. When they don't, they bring silence — and silence is expensive.

People will always find safety somewhere.

If they can't find it with you, they'll find it in side chats, exit interviews, or someone else's organization.

Your Challenge

When someone shares an unfinished idea this week, resist the urge to critique.

Say, "Let's explore that."

Then share one of your own half-baked thoughts in return.

That's how safety starts — small, genuine, and real.

Cheeky Reminder:

If your team's afraid to fail, they're not
innovating — they're surviving.
And survival mode is no place for great ideas.

7

TRUST

The Invisible Glue Holding It All Together

Trust isn't a warm, fuzzy feeling — it's infrastructure.

It's the invisible framework that keeps everything else from falling apart.

Without trust, teams spiral into overthinking and self-protection.

With it, work flows — less guarding, more doing.

In low-trust teams, people overthink, over-explain, and wait for approval.

In high-trust teams, they just get on with it.

One crawls; the other flies.

So how do you build trust — and more importantly, how do you keep from smashing it to pieces?

Why Trust Matters

- **The Constant:** Consistency beats charisma.
  Example: Trust isn't built in grand gestures; it's built in the small stuff — the follow-ups, the "I'll get back to you Friday" promises that actually happen.
- **Why It Matters:** Reliability is louder than any pep talk. People don't need inspiration as much as they need someone who does what they said they would.

~~~~

- **The Principle:** Transparency is oxygen.
  Example: "We're going this direction because…" is clarity. "Because I said so" is control.
- **Why It Matters:** When people understand the *why*, they'll walk through uncertainty with you. When they don't, they start guessing — and those guesses rarely flatter you.

~~~~

- **The Reminder:** Credit is currency.
  Example: Give public recognition for great work. The moment you take credit for someone else's success, you've filed for trust bankruptcy.
- **Why It Matters:** People forgive mistakes faster than they forgive being erased.

~~~~

- **The Practice:** Humanity wins every time.
  Example: Admit when you're wrong. Apologize when you mess up. Ask how people are — and mean it.
- **Why It Matters:** Leaders who act like humans earn loyalty. Leaders who act like robots earn compliance.

Cheeky Insight

If your Wi-Fi dropping gets louder
applause than your leadership updates,
it's not the signal that's weak.

The Trust Battery

Think of trust like a battery — it charges slowly and drains fast.

Every interaction either fills it or fries it.

Follow through on a promise? Charge.

Cancel a one-on-one with no explanation? Drain.

Ask for input, then act on it? Charge.

Ghost someone's urgent message for three days? Big drain.

Trust isn't about perfection; it's about *patterns*.

Picture two teammates:

- Alice delivers on time, helps others, remembers birthdays. Her battery hums at 90%. When she misses a deadline, people shrug — rare event.
- Bob runs late, forgets follow-ups, blames "calendar confusion." His battery's at 20%. When he slips again, no one's shocked.

Now imagine Bob turns it around. He follows through, communicates, stays steady. The battery climbs. But if he backslides? It drains twice as fast.

Trust grows slowly and evaporates instantly — like Monday-morning coffee.

How to Destroy Trust
(and Quickly)

- **Red Flag:** Micromanagement screams, "I don't trust you."
  Example: A manager who hovers over every detail doesn't create accountability — just anxiety.
- **Why It Matters:** When people feel watched, they stop taking initiative.

~~~

- **Warning:** Broken promises break people.
  Example: You promised feedback and never sent it. Small to you, defining to them.
- **Why It Matters:** Trust is made of micro-moments; lose enough and the whole structure collapses.

~~~

- **Reality Check:** Playing favorites poisons culture.
  Example: Rewarding the same few people regardless of effort tells everyone else, "Don't bother."
- **Why It Matters:** Fairness builds loyalty. Favors build resentment.

~~~

- **The Trap:** Gossip corrodes credibility.
  Example: If your team hears you vent about others, they assume you do it about *them*.
- **Why It Matters:** Trust doesn't die dramatically, it dies in whispers.

Cheeky Tip

If "Did you hear what the boss said?" sends people into panic, the boss might be you.

The Fallout of Broken Trust

When trust cracks, everything slows. Communication turns cautious. Meetings become performances instead of problem-solving.

People stop caring about *what's next* because they're still nursing *what just happened.*

Turnover climbs. Innovation stalls. Culture becomes all talk, no truth.

Real-World Glimpse:

Remember the company that blasted, *"We're all in this together"* right before layoffs?

That's trust erosion in real time.

Or the manager who keeps canceling one-on-ones "because something came up."

That *something* is trust walking out the door.

Rebuilding Trust

- **First Step:** Start small, stay steady.
  Example: Deliver on tiny promises first — "I'll get back to you by end of day" is where restoration begins.
- **Why It Matters:** Every kept promise is a brick in the rebuild.

~~~~~

- **Next Move:** Listen without defending.
  Example: Ask, "What can I do better?" and fight the urge to explain.
- **Why It Matters:** People start trusting again when they feel heard — not managed.

~~~~~

- **Key Practice:** Apologies are actions, not words.
  Example: "I messed that up, and here's how I'm fixing it" lands very differently from "My bad."
- **Why It Matters:** Accountability isn't confession; it's correction.

~~~~~

- **Ground Rule:** Be present when it matters most.
  Example: Show up when someone's struggling — not just when they're shining.
- **Why It Matters:** Consistency in hard moments cements credibility.

Cheeky Insight

If your apology includes "if anyone was offended," you're still doing it wrong.

Micro-Case Study:
Rebuilding Trust Brick by Brick

After a messy layoff, a SaaS company went all-in on transparency. Weekly all-hands turned into open forums. Leaders shared what they knew, admitted what they didn't, and invited real questions — even the uncomfortable ones.

It wasn't instant, but trust came back.

Two years later, when layoffs hit again, employees didn't panic. They *understood*.

That's what honesty earns you: calm in chaos.

Reflection Section

When trust breaks in your organization, how — and by whom — is it rebuilt?

Leader Lens

Trust is fragile but fixable.

It isn't built by speeches; it's built by being the same person every time people interact with you.

Reliability *is* leadership.

Notes

List two behaviors that charge your trust battery — and one that drains it.

What would happen if you flipped that ratio this week?

Wrapping It Up

Trust isn't earned once; it's earned daily.

It's not built through a single act of loyalty but through thousands of micro-moments of follow-through.

When you keep your word, show up when it's inconvenient, and lead without hidden agendas, people stop guarding themselves, and start giving you their best.

Teams that thrive don't just share goals; they share belief in each other.

They know that if one person stumbles, someone else will catch them.

That's the invisible glue that turns coworkers into collaborators.

⭐ *Your Challenge* ⭐

Find one opportunity this week to over-deliver on a promise, no matter how small.

Those are the deposits that rebuild belief.

⟜➤ Quick Note Before We Keep Going

If this chapter feels familiar, good.

The best leaders don't master fifty new things — they repeat five essential ones until they stick.

That's how trust, safety, and care work: not as initiatives, but as habits.

8

CARING

It's Not Rocket Science,
But It's Everything

Here's the secret no one writes in the strategy decks:

Everything — culture, performance,
retention — starts with caring.

Not the performative, corporate "we value our people" kind.

Real, messy, human caring — the kind that notices, remembers, and follows through.

Caring isn't about grand gestures or flashy perks. It's about proving, in small, consistent ways, that people matter more than metrics. When leaders genuinely care, workplaces shift. Energy changes. People stop bracing and start believing.

Why Caring Matters

- **The Constant:** Caring builds loyalty faster than bonuses ever will.
  Example: A leader who remembers a birthday or checks in after a rough week sends a louder message than any corporate slogan: *You matter beyond your output.*
- **Why It Matters:** People stay where they feel valued. Appreciation is retention strategy disguised as kindness.

~~~~~

- **The Principle:** Caring fuels engagement.
  Example: A manager who asks, "What's one thing I can do to make your job easier?" doesn't just fix a workflow — they signal that wellbeing is on the agenda.
- **Why It Matters:** When people feel seen, they give you what you can't buy: effort, creativity, and commitment.

~~~~~

- **The Practice:** Caring inspires growth.
  Example: Instead of saying, "You're not ready for that role," a thoughtful leader says, "Here's what to work on so you can get there."
- **Why It Matters:** Support turns disappointment into direction.

Cheeky Insight

Caring isn't hard. Ignoring people is.
And it costs a lot more in turnover.

How to Show You Care
(Without a Budget or a Banner)

- **The Move:** Start small, stay consistent.
  Example: A simple "Good morning" or "How was your weekend?" takes seconds but signals presence. One leader began every meeting with brief personal check-ins — and within months, engagement quietly climbed.
- **Why It Matters:** Micro-moments compound. A pattern of attention becomes a culture of connection.

~~~~~

- **The Reminder:** Follow through.
  Example: A manager promises to review workload balance and actually does. Another forgets. Guess whose team stops talking?
- **Why It Matters:** Reliability is the professional love language.

~~~~~

- **The Habit:** Give feedback like you mean it.
  Example: "Here's what to improve — and how I'll help you get there" beats "Do better."
- **Why It Matters:** Feedback isn't criticism; it's investment.

~~~~~

- **The Shift:** Celebrate people, not just performance.
  Example: Ask about someone's art class, their kid's game, or their weekend hike. It's not small talk — it's connection.
- **Why It Matters:** When people feel known, they belong.

Cheeky Tip

If you're "too busy to care," you're not leading — you're managing chaos.

When Caring Goes Wrong

- **The Red Flag:** Performative caring backfires.
  Example: A company sends a "We care about mental health" email — then books five back-to-back Friday meetings.
- **Why It Matters:** Empty gestures breed cynicism faster than silence.

~~~

- **The Misstep:** One-size-fits-all caring misses the point.
  Example: Pizza parties for a burned-out team? Cute. But what they needed was a break.
- **Why It Matters:** Real care meets people where they are, not where it's convenient.

Cheeky Insight

If your compassion plan involves a sheet cake and a hashtag, start over.

Caring in Action

⬦ **The Leader Who Showed Up:** A regional manager called each remote team member weekly — no agenda, just connection. The calls lasted minutes. The impact lasted months.

⬦ **The Company That Listened:** After employees voiced burnout, leadership trimmed meetings, brought in counselors, and added wellness stipends. Productivity rose — but more importantly, people exhaled.

⬦ **The Thoughtful Manager:** During a brutal quarter, one leader wrote handwritten thank-you notes highlighting specific contributions. Morale rebounded faster than any bonus could manage.

Micro-Case Study:
The Power of Giving a Damn

A COO began every meeting with one question:
"How's your energy today?"

At first, everyone rolled their eyes. But weeks later, they started answering honestly. "Running low." "Feeling stretched." "Pretty good, actually."

That five-second ritual became the team's pulse check.

Performance climbed — not because the metrics changed, but because the people did.

Caring wasn't a program. It was a practice.

Reflection Section

Who made you feel seen at work?

What exactly did they do — and how could you pass that forward?

Leader Lens

Caring isn't soft; it's strategic.

Presence, curiosity, and empathy aren't extras — they're the behaviors that turn compliance into belonging.

Notes

Write down one caring act you could take today.
No budget. No announcement. Just intent.

Wrapping It Up

Caring isn't complicated — but it is revolutionary.

When people feel connected and supported, they show up differently. They collaborate more. They stay longer. They give their best — not because they have to, but because they *want to.*

This isn't about motivational posters or "Employee Appreciation Days."

It's about small, consistent choices: asking one more question, keeping one more promise, noticing one more human.

✦ *Your Challenge* ✦

Ask yourself: *Do people know I care, or am I assuming they do?* If you're assuming, you've got work to do.

Cheeky Reminder

Giving a crap is free.
The ROI is enormous.
Skip the pizza party — try being human instead.

9

THE ENERGY EQUATION

Leading Without Burning Out

Here's a radical truth most leaders learn the hard way:

You can't pour from an empty cup — or lead from an exhausted mind.

The Energy Equation is simple but relentless:

$$Energy = Capacity + Intention.$$

If your capacity is depleted or your intention misplaced, you'll burn bright — then burn out.

And yet, in too many workplaces, exhaustion is worn like a badge of honor.

"Busy" becomes a personality trait.

"I'll sleep when this project's done" becomes the corporate anthem.

But here's the thing — burned-out leaders create burned-out teams.

Your energy sets the tone more than any memo or mission statement ever will.

Why Energy Matters

- **The Constant:** Energy is contagious — for better or worse. *Example:* A manager who enters every meeting frazzled, sighing, and half-listening teaches everyone else to do the same. Another who starts with presence and humor shifts the entire room's rhythm.
- **Why It Matters:** Leadership is an emotional amplifier. Your mood multiplies faster than your instructions.

~~~~~

- **The Reality:** Burnout kills creativity and trust faster than failure ever will. *Example:* A founder running on fumes keeps changing direction mid-project, confusing her team and draining morale.
- **Why It Matters:** When you're stuck in survival mode, every decision becomes reactive — and everyone feels it.

~~~~~

- **The Reminder:** Sustainable leadership is a discipline, not a luxury. *Example:* One executive blocked "Think Time" on her calendar every Friday — nonnegotiable. She called it her *refuel ritual.* Within months, she was calmer, sharper, and her team's turnover dropped by half.
- **Why It Matters:** Rest isn't indulgent — it's strategic. You're not a machine, and even machines need maintenance.

Cheeky Insight

If you brag about how little you sleep, you're not a high performer — you're a hazard with a laptop.

The Anatomy of Energy

Energy has three layers, and great leaders protect all of them.

1. Physical Energy — *The Foundation*

- **The Move:** Eat real food. Move your body. Sleep like it's your job.
  Example: One VP introduced "Walking 1:1s." Same discussions, fewer headaches, better ideas.
- **Why It Matters:** When your body's running on empty, your brain files for bankruptcy.

2. Emotional Energy — *The Pulse*

- **The Shift:** Separate what's urgent from what's important.
  Example: A leader who reacts to every Slack ping like a fire alarm teaches panic. One who pauses before replying teaches poise.
- **Why It Matters:** Emotional regulation isn't stoicism — it's stewardship. It keeps everyone else from drowning in your wake.

3. Relational Energy — *The Multiplier*

- **The Practice:** Surround yourself with people who recharge you, not drain you.
  Example: A leader began tracking who energized or exhausted her after meetings. Then she adjusted her schedule. The result? More patience, more creativity, fewer mystery migraines.
- **Why It Matters:** Culture runs on human batteries. Don't let energy vampires lead the charge.

Cheeky Tip ⌁

"It's just been a busy season" is what every burned-out leader says right before they make a terrible decision.

The Hidden Energy Leaks

Even the best leaders lose energy in sneaky ways. Watch for these drains:

- ◈ **Overcommitment:** Saying yes to everything means saying no to excellence.
- ◈ **Unclear Boundaries:** If your team's "quick question" window is 24/7, you're not managing — you're melting.
- ◈ **Performative Productivity:** Staying "visible" online just to look busy is corporate cosplay.
- ◈ **Neglected Renewal:** You wouldn't skip refueling your car mid-road trip. Why are you skipping your recharge?

Example: One remote company required cameras on at all times. Morale tanked. Creativity flatlined. When leadership dropped the rule and encouraged offline time, productivity *rose.*

- **Why It Matters:** Visibility doesn't equal value. Trust the work, not the webcam.

Cheeky Insight
If your idea of self-care is closing your laptop five minutes early, you're overdue for an energy intervention.

Refueling the Right Way

1. Protect Your Margins.

Schedule white space. Energy can't thrive in back-to-back meetings.

Example: A director blocked 15-minute buffers between meetings. Soon, the whole team copied the habit — burnout dropped, focus rose.

2. Model Balance Out Loud.

If you tell your team to rest but send midnight emails, they'll follow what you do, not what you say.

Example: A COO began tagging late-night messages "For Tomorrow." Engagement rose, not because she worked less, but because people felt permission to pause.

3. Design Work with Flow.

Match peak energy to high-focus tasks.

Example: A creative agency moved brainstorms to mornings when energy peaked and saved admin work for the afternoon. Productivity soared — so did morale.

Cheeky Tip

You don't need a wellness app. You need boundaries, daylight, and sleep.

Micro-Case Study:
The Burnout Rebrand

A mid-sized consulting firm was losing talent fast.

Deadlines were constant, praise was rare, and "urgent" meant "everything."

Leadership finally flipped the script:

- ▶ Fridays after 2 p.m. became "No-Meeting Zones."
- ▶ Teams rotated coverage for predictable downtime.
- ▶ Managers were trained to spot early burnout signals.

Six months later, turnover dropped 25%, engagement jumped 40%, and people started smiling again on Zoom.

Turns out, rest scales better than panic.

Reflection Section

Where are your biggest energy leaks — your calendar, your habits, or your mindset?

What's one boundary you could set this week to protect your energy and set an example for your team?

Leader Lens

Energy isn't just personal — it's cultural.

When leaders normalize reflection, rest, and recovery, they build teams that last.

Notes

List one habit that recharges you and one that drains you. Now block time for the first and a boundary for the second.

Wrapping It Up

Leadership isn't a sprint — it's a marathon through unpredictable terrain.

If you don't manage your energy, your brilliance becomes a liability.

Audit your week like a CFO of your own capacity:

What's yielding a return? What's draining your reserves?

Because the truth is simple: you can't lead transformation if you're running on fumes.

Cheeky Reminder

You're not paid to burn out beautifully.
You're paid to lead sustainably.
Charge your batteries — and your people will, too.

Part Two

FROM THINKING TO DOING

Y ou've rethought what leadership means.

You've unlearned the noise, questioned the "rules," and (hopefully) started noticing that great leadership isn't about having all the answers — it's about asking better questions, more often.

Now it's time to move.

Section I challenged how you *see* leadership.
Section II challenges how you *practice* it.

This is where philosophy meets behavior — where people-first thinking becomes people-first systems.

No new buzzwords. No color-coded frameworks. Just real, imperfect implementation.

Because insight without action is just a nice thought. And nice thoughts don't change teams.

Here's the reality: building a healthy organization isn't about sweeping overhauls or overnight transformations.

It's about small, visible choices — how you hire, onboard, communicate, give feedback, recognize effort, and help people grow.

The quiet, consistent habits that define culture when no one's watching.

In this section, you'll turn *why* into *how*.

You'll design work that actually works.

You'll build teams that thrive without needing a hero at the helm.

And you'll prove that operational excellence and human decency aren't opposites — they're partners.

Cheeky Reminder

The best culture change doesn't start with an initiative.
It starts with someone deciding to do one thing
better on Monday.

So let's get practical.

Let's get a little uncomfortable.

And let's make leadership look less like a performance — and more like progress.

10

THE MYTH OF
THE PERFECT CANDIDATE

Most job descriptions are wish lists wrapped in jargon.
"Must have 10 years of experience, advanced degrees, and the ability to walk on water."

Please.

Somewhere along the way, hiring turned into fantasy casting — as if the right person will appear, perfectly credentialed, perfectly polished, and perfectly exhausted from meeting your impossible expectations.

Newsflash: the "perfect candidate" doesn't exist.

The best hires rarely check every box. They bring curiosity, grit, and the ability to figure things out as they go.

Why the Perfect Candidate Doesn't Exist

- **The Reality:** Credentials aren't character.
  Example: You can find someone with a decade of experience and zero initiative — or someone with less experience and limitless drive.
- **The Ripple Effect:** Skills can be taught. Grit can't. When you hire for heart and mindset, you future-proof your team.

- **The Lesson:** Perfection kills potential.
  Example: A startup rewrote "10+ years required" to "proven ability to deliver results." It opened the door to overlooked talent — and they hired a rock star who'd been ignored everywhere else.
- **Why It Matters:** Potential creates momentum. Perfection creates stagnation.

- **The Reminder:** "Culture fit" isn't sameness.
  Example: A retail manager with no fintech experience became a top performer at a digital bank because their empathy and service instincts translated across industries.
- **Why It Matters:** When you hire for shared values instead of identical résumés, you build loyalty and innovation.

Cheeky Insight

If your job description reads like it was written by a robot, don't be shocked when only robots apply.

How to Hire for What Actually Matters

Ask better questions.

Instead of "What are your strengths?" ask "Tell me about a time you learned something the hard way."

>>> *Resilience and reflection reveal more than polished answers ever will.*

Use real people — not just algorithms.

A 10-minute human conversation uncovered creative problem-solving that the ATS had filtered out.

>>> *Computers don't hire humans. People do. Act like it.*

Sell your organization like it's worth joining.

Add a "Why You'll Thrive Here" section to job postings that describes how you invest in growth, recognition, and flexibility.

>>> *Top talent is interviewing you too. If you can't explain why they should pick you, they won't.*

Cheeky Tip ☞
"We're a dynamic team leveraging synergies" isn't a flex — it's a cry for help.

When Hiring Goes Wrong

Over-filtering kills diversity — and creativity.

A company eliminated applicants without four-year degrees — and missed someone who later became a competitor's COO.

>>> *Narrow definitions of 'qualified' shrink your future before it starts.*

Complexity costs credibility.

A candidate spent 90 minutes on an application, only to receive an auto-reject five minutes later.

>>> *Your hiring process is your first impression. If it's painful, they'll pass.*

Cheeky Insight

If Einstein wouldn't make it past your ATS, it's not filtering for brilliance — it's filtering for boredom.

Hiring in Action

◇ **The Food Truck Operator:** A growing company hired a former food truck owner with zero corporate experience. Within weeks, he streamlined logistics and saved ten hours a week.

◇ **The Career Changer:** A teacher became a customer success manager — and brought empathy and clarity that reshaped client relationships.

◇ **The Wild Card:** A bartender turned team lead rebuilt morale and retention in a division known for turnover.

Cheeky Tip

"Unqualified" people often turn out to be your most qualified humans.

Micro-Case Study:
From Unicorns to Humans

At a New York–based company, HR realized their "perfect candidate" obsession was choking the pipeline.

They rewrote job ads around curiosity and values, not tenure.

The result? Broader reach, faster hires, and a team that actually enjoyed working together.

One recruiter put it best:

"We stopped hunting unicorns and started finding people who gave a rip."

Reflection Section

What types of candidates have you overlooked because they didn't fit your checklist?

What might you gain if you hired for trajectory instead of tradition?

Leader Lens

The best leaders hire for *who someone can become,* not just *who they've been.*

Train for skills. Screen for values.

Build people who grow with you — not away from you.

Notes

Write one interview question that reveals character or curiosity — then use it in your next conversation.

_____

_____

_____

_____

_____

Wrapping It Up

The "perfect candidate" is a myth.
But the _right_ one? They're probably already in your inbox.
When you hire for curiosity and growth, you're not collecting résumés — you're shaping culture. Great teams don't happen by chance; they're built by people who care enough to design them.

Your Challenge

Look past the paper.
In your next hiring decision, choose the person who asks the best questions — not the one with the longest list of answers.

Cheeky Reminder

Perfect is predictable.
People are powerful. Hire humans.

11

WHY YOUR ONBOARDING SUCKS

(and How to Fix it)

You found your person — sharp, curious, and probably wondering if you're the real deal.

Now comes the test: can you make their first day feel like possibility, not paperwork?

Day one should feel like joining something that matters — not like surviving a corporate obstacle course.

Yet somehow, most onboarding feels like a punishment disguised as a process. You get the login, the handbook, the compliance videos, and maybe a half-hearted "Welcome aboard!" Slack message. Then… silence.

Onboarding isn't about forms. It's about first impressions.

It's your organization's moment to prove that *"people-first"* wasn't a recruiting slogan — it's how you actually operate.

Good onboarding builds confidence.

Bad onboarding builds exit plans.

Why Onboarding Matters

- **The Constant:** Onboarding is your culture's first test. *Example:* You can preach "people-first" all you want, but if someone's first day involves a broken laptop, missing badge, and zero direction, the message is clear: *You're on your own.*
- **Why It Matters:** First impressions become lasting assumptions. People decide if they belong within days — not quarters.

~~~

- **The Lesson:** Great onboarding outperforms great recruiting. *Example:* A company spent six months finding the "perfect fit," then lost them in six weeks because onboarding was a ghost town.
- **Why It Matters:** Recruiting attracts talent. Onboarding keeps it.

~~~

- **The Reminder:** It's not about perfection; it's about intention. *Example:* A handwritten note and an organized first-week plan beat any branded water bottle.
- **Why It Matters:** People remember how you made them feel — not what logo was on their notebook.

Cheeky Insight

Imagine wooing someone on a first date, then showing up distracted and half-dressed. That's bad onboarding energy.

How to Fix It
(Without Turning It Into a Circus)

Start before day one.

Send a short "We can't wait for you to start" email with setup details, warm intros, and an invite to their first team meeting.

>>> *Day one shouldn't be the first time they feel seen.*

Make it personal.

Use a quick "Get to Know Me" form — favorite coffee, work style, birthday. One leader even made team-curated welcome playlists.

>>> *Personalization isn't fluff; it's connection.*

Prioritize connection over compliance.

Trade a few policy presentations for cross-team coffee chats. It's less *orientation*, more *integration*.

>>> *People don't fall in love with companies — they connect with people.*

Extend the runway.

Build a 30/60/90-day plan with learning milestones and regular check-ins. Send a quick "30-day win" note from leadership to celebrate progress.

>>> *Ongoing attention says 'We're invested.' Silence says 'Good luck.'*

Ditch the sink-or-swim mentality.

Pair every new hire with a mentor or buddy. Structure builds safety; safety builds confidence.

>>> *No one thrives while treading water — and the best talent won't stay to learn how.*

Cheeky Tip ⌔

If your onboarding motto is "figure it out," congrats — you're onboarding future quitters.

When Onboarding Goes Wrong

Disorganization kills excitement.
A new hire spends day one waiting for IT to find their login. By day two, they're questioning life choices.
>>> *Chaos signals carelessness. You can't claim excellence while winging the basics.*

Over-engineering kills authenticity.
Ten hours of mandatory videos, zero human conversation.
>>> *Efficiency is great, but connection is what sticks.*

Cheeky Insight ⌔

If you measure onboarding success by completion rates instead of connection, you've missed the point.

Onboarding in Action

◇ **A Healthcare Nonprofit:** Replaced a PowerPoint marathon with buddy programs, welcome kits, and weekly check-ins. Year-one retention jumped 35%.

- ◇ **A Startup:** Added "First Week Shoutouts" on Slack. One new hire said, "It felt like joining a team, not a machine."
- ◇ **A Remote Company:** Paired new hires with "culture buddies" who decoded unspoken norms — saving months of confusion.

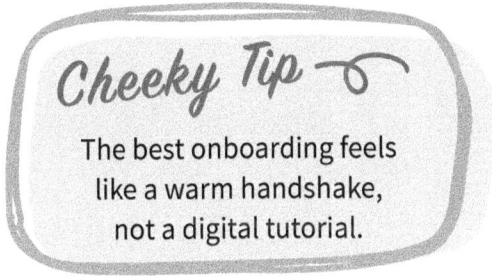

Cheeky Tip

The best onboarding feels like a warm handshake, not a digital tutorial.

Micro-Case Study:
Onboarding That Doesn't Suck

A healthcare nonprofit noticed their new hires looked more panicked than proud by day three. They scrapped the 47-slide welcome deck and built a "First 90 Days" roadmap with mentors, check-ins, and honest conversation.

One new employee said,

"It felt like they were waiting for me — not surprised I showed up."

Retention rose, morale soared, and HR finally stopped hiding under their desks.

Reflection Section

What message does your onboarding send — *"Welcome to the team"* or *"Good luck surviving"*?

What's one thing you could remove tomorrow to make week one feel more human?

Leader Lens

Onboarding isn't paperwork — it's storytelling.

Those first weeks are your chance to prove that *"people-first"* wasn't a tagline. It's a practice.

Notes

List two small touches that could make onboarding more personal — one before day one, one after week one.

Wrapping It Up

Onboarding isn't a formality; it's a first impression that echoes.

Every email, every login, every small gesture tells a story about who you are as an organization — and your new hires are listening closely.

When you get it right, you don't just retain people — you ignite belief.

People don't join companies; they join experiences.

If that experience begins with confusion or distance, the magic fades before it ever starts.

But when someone walks in and feels genuinely welcomed and supported, they don't just integrate — they invest.

Great onboarding isn't about swag or slogans. It's about trust built in real time.

It's your chance to say, *"You belong here, and we're glad you came."*

✦ *Your Challenge* ✦

Audit your onboarding like it's your own first day.

Where does it sparkle? Where does it stall?

Fix one thing this month that would make a new hire's first week unforgettable — for the right reasons.

Cheeky Reminder

Don't make people fall in love with your culture during recruiting only to ghost them on day one.

If "people-first" is your promise, onboarding is your proof.

12

THE ART OF EXPECTATION SETTING

We're Not Mind Readers

We've all been there — staring at someone's work, thinking, *"They should just know."*

Hate to break it to you: they never do.

One manager assumed her new hire would 'just know' how to prep for executive reviews — three missed slides later, both learned otherwise.

Expectation setting isn't optional; it's leadership oxygen.

Without it, teams waste energy chasing clarity that never comes.

With it, people understand what success looks like and how their work moves the mission forward.

When I once coached a team through a major product launch, everyone was working late, tense, and slightly panicked — until we realized no one actually knew what *"done"* meant. The moment we defined the deliverables and deadlines, the tension evaporated. Nothing else changed — just the clarity. And that's the point: people rarely need more effort; they need direction.

Clarity isn't micromanagement.

It's respect.

Why Expectation Setting Matters

- **The Principle:** Clarity drives confidence.
  Example: Saying "Just do your best" or "I'd expect more from someone at your level" is like giving directions by saying, "Head north-ish."
- **Why It Matters:** Ambiguity breeds anxiety. When people know what success looks like, they stop guessing and start delivering.

~~~~

- **The Constant:** Clear expectations build trust.
  Example: "I need this report by Friday — detailed enough for the team to decide next steps" sets purpose and boundaries. Compare that to "ASAP."
- **Why It Matters:** Clarity feels like care. It tells people their time and effort matter.

~~~~

- **The Lesson:** Expectations make feedback less awkward.
  Example: "The report hit the deadline but missed the detail" is easy to discuss when the target was clear.
- **Why It Matters:** Feedback becomes a conversation, not a courtroom.

Cheeky Insight

If your feedback starts with "I assumed you knew...," congratulations — you've just confessed to bad leadership.

How to Set Expectations That Stick

Be specific, not dramatic.

Instead of "Make this presentation amazing," try "Include three real client examples and one story that brings the data to life."

>>> *Specificity gives people something to aim for — not guess at.*

Connect the dots.

"Your analysis will shape next quarter's investment plan" beats "Run the report."

>>> *People care more when they see how their work matters.*

Write it down.

A shared doc or project tool beats "We talked about it last week, remember?"

>>> *Memory is not a management strategy.*

Confirm understanding.

"Can you recap next steps so I know I explained it clearly?" feels supportive, not condescending.

>>> *Clarification now saves cleanup later.*

Cheeky Tip

If their recap sounds like a completely different project, you didn't set expectations — you started a scavenger hunt.

When Expectations Go Wrong

Vague goals waste time.

"Improve engagement" means ten different things to ten different people.

>>> *If no one knows what winning looks like, don't expect victory.*

Moving goalposts destroy trust.

Changing priorities midweek without explanation breeds frustration.

>>> *People can adapt — they just need honesty to do it.*

Overload isn't leadership.

Assigning five "urgent" projects with one deadline isn't ambition — it's chaos in a blazer.

>>> *Overwhelm guarantees burnout, not brilliance.*

Expectation Setting in Action

✦ **Ritz-Carlton:** Every employee can spend up to $2,000 solving a guest issue — no approval needed. That's not policy; that's trust with parameters.

- **Google:** OKRs (Objectives and Key Results) link every role to company-wide outcomes — so no one's guessing what matters most.
- **Startup Win:** Weekly team check-ins to restate priorities cut missed deadlines in half and ended the "I didn't know that was due" chorus.

Micro-Case Study:
The Clarity Revolution

A creative agency swapped vague project briefs for bullet-pointed success criteria: purpose, deliverables, and "what 'done' looks like."

Designers stopped playing psychic. Revisions dropped. Deadlines stuck.

One employee summed it up best:

"Turns out we're great at our jobs — we just needed to know what the job was."

Reflection Section

When was the last time you clarified expectations — and actually got clarity back?

What one conversation this week could prevent a month of frustration?

Leader Lens

Expectation setting is the quiet superpower of effective leadership.

It prevents drama, builds trust, and replaces frustration with focus.

The best leaders don't assume alignment — they create it.

Notes

Pick one ongoing project. Write down what success actually looks like — in plain English. Then say it out loud.

Wrapping It Up

Expectation setting doesn't make you controlling.
It makes you credible.

When people know what success looks like, they rise to meet it.

When they don't, they fill the silence with guesswork, stress, and Slack messages that start with, "Hey, quick question…"

Clarity is kindness.

Alignment is power.

The best teams aren't the ones that hustle the hardest — they're the ones that know exactly what "good" means.

⭐ *Your Challenge* ⭐

Audit one goal, one meeting, or one deliverable this week.

Does everyone know what success looks like — or are they still guessing?

Spell it out.

Cheeky Reminder

If your team has to read your mind to make you happy, you don't need a miracle — you need better sentences.

(13)

FIX YOUR FEEDBACK LOOPS

Stop Ghosting People

You know that awkward silence after a big presentation — the one where everyone nods politely, avoids eye contact, and then... nothing?

That's what broken feedback loops feel like.

Once, I coached a leader who thought her silence was "giving space." Her team thought it was disappointment. By the time she followed up, half the team had mentally checked out. The lesson? Silence doesn't feel neutral. It feels like judgment.

Whether it's a job candidate, a team member, or a customer, silence kills momentum. Feedback isn't just a courtesy — it's the fuel that keeps growth and motivation alive.

Ghosting isn't a leadership style.

It's avoidance in business casual.

Why Feedback Loops Matter

- **The Principle:** Silence breeds assumptions.
  Example: A manager skips follow-up after a project. The team assumes it went fine — until two weeks later when they hear leadership hated it. Cue the quiet frustration and a promise to care a little less next time.
- **Why It Matters:** People fill silence with stories, and they're rarely generous ones.

~~~

- **The Lesson:** Feedback is a signal of respect.
  Example: "Here's what worked, here's what didn't, and here's what's next" models clarity. Saying nothing says, "You don't matter enough to know."
- **Why It Matters:** Feedback isn't criticism; it's connection.

~~~

- **The Constant:** Feedback isn't a moment — it's a system.
  Example: Teams that check in weekly on progress, obstacles, and wins outperform those that save everything for quarterly reviews.
- **Why It Matters:** Frequency builds comfort. Comfort builds candor. Candor builds everything else.

Cheeky Insight

If the only time people get feedback is at review season, you're not leading — you're hosting an annual surprise party. And no one likes those.

How to Create Feedback Loops That Actually Loop

Make it normal, not formal.

Start meetings with "What's one thing we learned this week?" or end with "What could we do better next time?"

>>> *When feedback becomes part of the rhythm, it loses its sting and gains its power.*

Respond, even when the answer is no.

A customer submits an idea. An employee pitches an improvement. A simple, "Thanks — here's what we can and can't do right now," shows respect.

>>> *Silence feels like dismissal. Response feels like recognition.*

Example in Action: One company created a Teams channel where leadership replied to every suggestion with short video updates. Engagement soared — and the guessing stopped.

Give feedback like you're investing, not inspecting.

"Here's what I noticed and what I think you can build on" beats "You missed the mark."

>>> *Feedback given with care unlocks motivation instead of defensiveness.*

Ask for feedback — and mean it.

"What's one thing I could do better as your leader?" is worth more than any engagement survey.

>>> *The best leaders close the loop by acting on what they hear.*

Example in Action: "You said meetings run long, so we're cutting them by 15 minutes." That's not just listening — it's leading.

Cheeky Tip

If you ask for feedback but flinch every time someone gives it, that's not culture — that's emotional whiplash.

When Feedback Goes Missing

1. **Ghosting:** You don't respond, so people stop trying.
2. **Vagueness:** "Good job" and "Needs improvement" aren't feedback — they're filler.
3. **Fear:** When feedback gets punished, it gets buried.

Example: A team once full of ideas went silent after a leader publicly mocked a suggestion. Culture doesn't die dramatically — it suffocates quietly.

Cheeky Insight

If your "open door policy" means ideas can come in but never leave, it's not a policy — it's a trapdoor.

The Ripple Effect of Great Feedback

When feedback flows freely, everything improves:

- Employees know where they stand.
- Customers know they're heard.
- Leaders know what's real.

Example: A retail company added "We Heard You" updates to customer emails — summarizing feedback themes and fixes. Returns dropped, reviews rose, and brand loyalty spiked.

Inside the company, leaders did the same with staff surveys — openly sharing what changed. Employees stopped seeing surveys as black holes and started seeing them as catalysts.

Why It Matters: When people see proof that speaking up leads to action, they speak up more. That's not a campaign, that's culture.

Micro-Case Study:
The Feedback Flip

A fintech startup banned ghosting — with candidates, clients, and employees. Everyone got closure.

Within six months, Glassdoor reviews improved, engagement climbed, and one "rejected" candidate became a paying customer.

Turns out, basic decency scales beautifully.

Reflection Section

Think of a time when someone gave you feedback that stuck — what made it land?

Now think of a time you were met with silence — what did that silence cost?

Leader Lens

Feedback is leadership in action.
It's not about being right — it's about staying real.
Ask. Listen. Respond. Repeat.

Notes

Write two ways you can make feedback a habit, not an event.

Wrapping It Up

Feedback is how we stay human at work.

It's not a management tool, it's a mirror.

It reflects what we value, how we communicate, and whether we mean all that "people-first" talk.

Closing the loop doesn't need a platform or a program. It just takes a pause — long enough to acknowledge effort, respond thoughtfully, or say thank you.

That's it.

Your Challenge

Pick one place where feedback has gone stale — your team, your process, your customer experience — and breathe life back into it this week.

Cheeky Reminder

If your "feedback culture" feels more like a black hole than a conversation, stop waiting for an orbit to form.

Say something.

Mean it.

Repeat.

14

ACCOUNTABILITY WITHOUT THE FEAR FACTOR

Most people tense up when they hear the word *accountability.* Somewhere along the way, it stopped meaning responsibility and started sounding like blame.

But accountability done right isn't about punishment, it's about clarity. You can't be "too nice" for accountability. Niceness without clarity is negligence with a smile.

Real accountability is shared ownership, consistent follow-through, and the radical act of caring enough to tell the truth.

When I once helped a department reset after a missed deadline, everyone pointed fingers. The turning point came when a senior leader said, "Here's what I could have done differently." The tension broke instantly. Once blame left the room, progress walked in.

At its best, accountability is simply keeping promises — to people and to purpose.

Cheeky Tip ✎

If your version of accountability sounds like an interrogation, congratulations — you're not leading a team, you're running a crime scene.

Why Accountability Matters

Accountability builds confidence, not control.

A manager says, "Here's what success looks like, how we'll measure it, and how I'll support you." Everyone leaves clear and calm.

>>> *Accountability without clarity is just anxiety in a nicer outfit.*

Consistency beats intensity.

Leaders who hold regular, low-drama check-ins build reliability. Teams stop guessing when feedback will come and start trusting the rhythm of the work.

>>> *Predictability creates safety. Randomness breeds panic.*

It starts at the top.

When leaders admit, "I dropped the ball," they model ownership that spreads faster than any policy ever could.

>>> *You can't demand accountability you don't demonstrate.*

Cheeky Insight

The fastest way to kill accountability is to make it one-directional. If your team is held to a standard leadership doesn't follow, expect eye rolls, not results.

How to Create Accountability Without the Fear

1. Set the Rules — Together

Let your team help define what success looks like.

Example: A nonprofit co-created a "success charter" outlining both deliverables and how they'd achieve them — respectfully and on time.

>>> *When people help set the rules, they own the results.*

2. Use Data, Not Drama

Stick to facts. Replace "You're not performing" with "Here's the metric we missed and what we can do differently."

Example: A retail manager launched short weekly "pulse huddles" to review key metrics — no blame, just fixes. Performance rose 30% in one quarter.

>>> *Facts calm. Drama inflames.*

3. Recognize Accountability in Action

Most companies only talk about accountability when things go wrong. Flip it.

Example: A tech firm introduced "Honest Moments" — quick shares of lessons learned from mistakes. Owning up became a badge of maturity, not shame.

>>> *When people see accountability earn respect, they lean into it.*

4. Build Systems That Back You Up

Accountability shouldn't rely on heroic managers. Let it live in your processes.

Example: A clear project-tracking tool made ownership visible and stopped passive-aggressive email chains before they started.

>>> *Systems protect relationships. Visibility builds fairness.*

5. Lead With Questions, Not Accusations

Curiosity changes the tone instantly.

Swap "Why didn't you?" for "What got in the way?" or "What support would have helped?"

>>> *Curiosity opens doors. Accusation slams them shut.*

Cheeky Tip

"Help me understand" is leadership shorthand for "I'm listening." Use it often.

When Accountability Goes Wrong

The Blame Olympics

Finger-pointing replaces problem-solving.

Example: After a failed project, leadership spends an hour finding fault instead of solutions. Soon, no one volunteers ideas.

>>> *When fear of blame outweighs the desire to fix things, innovation dies first.*

The Disappearing Manager
Preaches ownership, vanishes when deadlines slip.
>>> *Double standards destroy credibility. People copy what they see, not what they hear.*

The "Nice" Leader Who Avoids It All
Avoiding accountability to spare feelings doesn't make you kind — it makes you unclear.
Example: A manager lets missed deadlines slide to "keep morale up." Instead, resentment grows and top performers burn out.
>>> *Real kindness is honest, not evasive.*

You can't be "too nice" for accountability. Niceness without clarity is negligence with a smile.

Success Stories:
Clarity That Changed the Game

- ◇ **The Startup That Ditched Fear:** Replaced formal reviews with monthly alignment chats asking two questions — "What's working?" and "What's blocking you?" Performance and morale skyrocketed.
- ◇ **The School District Win:** A superintendent introduced a "feedback compact" outlining shared commitments — direct, respectful, specific. Discipline issues dropped by half.
- ◇ **The Team That Made It Fun:** A marketing agency launched "Accountability Bingo." Every time someone owned an issue or fixed one proactively, they marked a square. Accountability became something to play, not fear.

Micro-Case Study:
The Blame Detox

A healthcare organization replaced tense "incident reviews" with "learning rounds."

The question changed from *"Who messed up?"* to *"What broke?"*

Within months, error reports increased (a good sign), morale improved, and saying "It's my fault" stopped sounding like a confession and started sounding like courage.

Reflection Section

Think of a time you avoided holding someone accountable. What were you protecting — your comfort or their growth?

Leader Lens

Accountability is empathy in action.

It's giving people clarity, not criticism — support, not shame.

Notes

Write one situation where accountability feels uncomfortable — and how you could approach it with curiosity instead of fear.

Wrapping It Up

Accountability isn't the enemy of compassion; it's an ally.

It's not punishment — it's partnership.

It's saying, *"I believe you can do this, and I care enough to help you get there."*

Lead with honesty and steadiness, and accountability stops being scary. It becomes empowering.

Your Challenge

Have one direct conversation you've been avoiding.

State the facts.

Ask what support's needed.

Then follow through.

Cheeky Reminder

Accountability doesn't appear by magic.
It takes conversations, systems, and
consistent follow-through.
Be clear.
Be fair.
Be steady.

15

PERFORMANCE MANAGEMENT THAT DOESN'T SUCK

B e honest — the annual review is the workplace equivalent of a root canal. Painful. Awkward. Followed by a polite "thanks" and a promise to "do better next year." (Spoiler: they won't.)

The problem isn't *that* we measure performance; it's *what* we measure.

When success is reduced to numbers, we reward results over behavior and miss the quiet signals that actually sustain success.

If your top performer leaves a trail of burned-out teammates behind them, your system isn't working — it's enabling.

Why Traditional Reviews Fail

Measuring only output is outdated.

Sarah crushes quotas and morale in equal measure. She hoards leads, claims credit, and treats collaboration like a spectator sport. On paper, she's a star. In reality, she's a storm.

>>> *Toxic "high performers" cost more than they produce.*

Reviews should drive growth, not fear.

The annual "surprise feedback" meeting isn't a process — it's a plot twist. Real conversations happen regularly, with context and care.

>>> *People grow through dialogue, not verdicts.*

Cheeky Tip

If "Let's circle back at your review" makes people tense, the issue isn't your team — it's your system.

How to Measure What Actually Matters

Blend results with behaviors.

Recognize *how* people deliver, not just *what* they deliver. A developer who mentors others adds as much value as the one who ships the most code.

>>> *When kindness counts, it multiplies.*

Make fairness visible.

If promotions always go to the loudest voices, quiet stars will find other stages.

Example: A peer-nominated "Values in Action" award ensures recognition flows sideways, not just top-down.

>>> *Consistency builds trust — and trust keeps talent.*

Be transparent.

Share what "great" looks like before you judge anyone for missing it. Hold short, frequent check-ins as priorities evolve.

>>> *Surprise belongs at birthday parties, not in reviews.*

Cheeky Insight

If "meets expectations" is your highest compliment, congratulations — you've turned mediocrity into a metric.

Modern Performance in Practice

Make feedback real-time.

Quick Slack kudos or short "mini-reviews" after projects keep feedback normal, not nerve-wracking.

Example: A marketing team's shared "Win Wall" became the most-visited channel — and productivity quietly climbed.

>>> *Recognition loses power when it's delayed.*

Focus on development, not damage control.

Ask, "Where do you want to grow next quarter?" instead of "Where did you fall short?"

Example: A manager built 90-day growth tracks for each team member. Promotions followed — and so did confidence.*

>>> *When performance becomes a map, people stop fearing it and start owning it.*

Gather feedback 360°.

Peers and direct reports often see what leaders can't.

Example: Anonymous peer input with one rule — feedback must be useful. "More patient in meetings" beats "less annoying."

>>> *Multiple perspectives reduce blind spots.*

Celebrate the Right Wins

Performance management isn't only about correction; it's about amplification.

Replace "Employee of the Month" with "Values in Action."

"Thanks to Marcus for mentoring new hires" hits harder than "Congrats, you did your job."

>>> *Recognition drives repetition. What you celebrate, you multiply.*

Cheeky Tip

Donuts are nice. Genuine appreciation lasts longer than frosting.

Micro-Case Study:
Measuring What Matters

A tech company discovered its top earner was also its biggest morale killer.

They ditched the "numbers-only" model and added collaboration, curiosity, and consistency to the scorecard.

Six months later: quieter chaos, sharper creativity, and higher revenue.

Turns out happy teams outperform jerks.

Reflection Section

Which behaviors get rewarded in your world — the helpful or the heroic?

If you stopped tracking numbers for a week, how would you know who's thriving?

Leader Lens

Performance systems don't shape culture — they expose it.

Design one that rewards the right things, and you'll never need slogans about teamwork.

Notes

List two behaviors you want to see more of — and one practical way you'll start noticing them.

Wrapping It Up

Performance management doesn't have to suck. It just has to remember people.

When you reward only the loudest voices, you silence the best thinkers.

When you measure only outputs, you miss the inputs that make them possible.

Great leaders design systems that see the whole person — not just the outcomes, but the impact of how those outcomes are achieved.

Your Challenge

Review your current metrics.

Do they reinforce the culture you claim to value — or the one you quietly tolerate?

Adjust accordingly.

Cheeky Reminder

If your performance template still says
"rank and rate," it's not a review, it's reality TV.
Cancel the season. Start fresh.

(16)

RECOGNITION

Fueling Performance with Appreciation

et's get something straight: everyone wants to feel seen.

From the intern triple-checking a spreadsheet to the CEO pulling an all-nighter before the board meeting, recognition is the universal language of motivation.

Yet most companies still treat it as a "nice-to-have," not a "need-to-do."

Recognition isn't plaques, pizza parties, or "Employee of the Month" photos curling on a forgotten wall. It's saying, *"You matter. What you did mattered."*

When done right, recognition becomes a performance multiplier — not a morale Band-Aid.

Why Recognition Matters

Recognition drives results more effectively than pressure ever could.

A sales manager publicly praises a creative client pitch. The team doesn't just clap — they start thinking bigger.

>>> *Gratitude outperforms grind every time.*

Recognition keeps your best people.

A tech firm introduced "Recognition Fridays," where peers nominate each other for weekly wins. Retention climbed, recruiting costs dropped, and engagement finally felt genuine.

>>> *Appreciation costs little. Replacing talent costs plenty.*

Recognition fuels purpose.

A nonprofit director tells a coordinator, "Your work secured housing for fifty families this month." Suddenly, the late nights make sense.

>>> *Purpose is built through acknowledgment, not Power-Points.*

Cheeky Tip

If your recognition strategy begins and ends with "Employee of the Month," congratulations — you've turned appreciation into paperwork.

How to Recognize — and Mean It

Be timely.

Recognition delayed is recognition denied.

A team launched a "Win Wall" where people post weekly shoutouts — from landing a client to surviving a tough sprint. Every name says, *"We see you."*

>>> *The faster you recognize effort, the faster it multiplies.*

Make it personal.

"Great job" is the fast-food version of feedback — quick, cheap, forgettable. Try, "Your attention to detail saved us hours."

One leader even sent handwritten notes: "You saved the timeline this week — and my sanity."

>>> *People remember sincerity, not slogans.*

Be consistent.

Start meetings with a "recognition round." Ask who made someone's day easier.

A global org launched peer-to-peer kudos credits redeemable for charity donations or time off. Recognition became part of the rhythm, not a random act.

>>> *Consistency turns appreciation into culture.*

Tie it to values.

If collaboration is a core value, highlight the employees who cross silos to make it happen.

>>> *When recognition reflects values, it reinforces them.*

Cheeky Insight

If your team can predict exactly when recognition is coming, it's too scripted to matter. Surprise wins loyalty — and hearts.

When Recognition Goes Wrong

Too much fluff kills impact.

"Great job opening that email!" isn't praise, it's parody. When you over-celebrate the obvious, you dilute genuine gratitude.

Forgetting the team does the same kind of damage. Praising only the project lead while ignoring the people who made it happen screams hierarchy over humanity. Recognition works best when it travels sideways, not just top-down.

And vagueness? That's the fastest way to make appreciation feel like autopilot. "Good job on the project" fades. "Your follow-through with the vendor kept us on schedule" lands — because it shows you were actually paying attention.

If your "thank you" could be copy-pasted to anyone, it's not gratitude — it's filler dressed as leadership.

Recognition in Action

◇ **Starbucks — Green Apron Awards:** Celebrates employees who embody the brand mission of "inspiring and nurturing the human spirit." Their stories circulate company-wide, turning mission into movement.

- **GE — "Above and Beyond" Program:** Encourages peer-to-peer recognition for living company values, with rewards that range from gift cards to dinners with leadership.
- **Start-Up Shoutout:** A marketing agency celebrates micro-moments — like an intern catching a $50,000 typo. That intern? Now full-time.

Micro-Case Study:
Recognition That Resonates

A logistics firm gave every employee $25 per month to appreciate a peer however they wanted — coffee, cards, small gifts.

Recognition skyrocketed. Even accounting smiled.

Reflection Section

When was the last time someone made you feel seen?
What exactly did they do — and how could you do the same for someone else?

Leader Lens

Recognition isn't a side dish; it's the main course.
Specific, timely, and authentic appreciation fuels performance more reliably than any bonus.

Notes

Write down two people who deserve recognition this week — and how you'll show it.

Wrapping It Up

Recognition isn't just "good vibes." It's the infrastructure of loyalty.

When people feel valued, they exceed expectations without being asked.

The challenge isn't *knowing* recognition matters — it's *doing* it with consistency and heart.

Your Challenge

Audit your recognition habits.

Are they heartfelt or halfhearted? Routine or real?

Because people remember how you made them feel long after they forget what you said.

Cheeky Reminder

If you think gratitude is optional, wait until your best performer quits — and thanks everyone *else* on LinkedIn. Too late. Say it now.

17

STOP BABYSITTING

Start Empowering

Remember that thing you *say* you give your team but can't resist taking back?

Yeah — autonomy.

Micromanagement is the silent killer of creativity and confidence. It's often disguised as "staying in the loop" or "just making sure we're aligned."

This chapter is your permission slip (and gentle shove) to stop hovering and start leading.

Because empowered employees don't just follow instructions — they take ownership.

Autonomy Isn't Chaos — It's Confidence

Some leaders hear *autonomy* and picture employees running wild, playing ping-pong while deadlines burn.

That's not autonomy — that's poor leadership hygiene.

True autonomy lives in the sweet spot between freedom and clarity — where people know what success looks like and have the space to figure out how to get there.

Example: A marketing team ditched its top-down approval chain and gave project leads full authority within set budgets and timelines.

The result? Faster campaigns, fewer bottlenecks, and a surge of creativity.

Reality Check: Autonomy without clarity is chaos. Autonomy with direction? That's where innovation shows up early and stays late.

Cheeky Tip

If your team needs your signature for every $50 purchase, you're not empowering — you're babysitting.

Accountability Without the Helicopter

People crave freedom *and* structure. They want ownership, not abandonment. Here's how to balance both without losing your mind:

- **The Shift:** Set clear expectations.
  A financial firm started every project with "success statements" — concise, outcome-based summaries that aligned everyone before kickoff. Rework dropped by 40%.

>>> *Clarity is the scaffolding of autonomy. You can't empower people who don't know what success looks like.*

- **The Shift:** Check in — don't hover.
  A manager replaced constant Teams pings with weekly one-on-ones focused on barriers, wins, and needs. Satisfaction soared.

>>> *Oversight isn't the same as overpresence. Trust needs breathing room.*

- **The Shift:** Use systems that support, not surveil.
  A product team introduced shared dashboards so progress stayed visible without micromanagement. Visibility stayed high; anxiety dropped.

>>> *Tools should enable confidence, not compliance.*

Cheeky Insight

You're leading adults, not interns. Let them stretch — maybe stumble — and learn. That's how growth happens.

How to Balance Empowerment and Oversight

Let's not kid ourselves: sometimes people make bad calls. And no, you don't need to let your business catch fire for the sake of "empowerment." The trick is balance.

1. Set Guardrails That Guide

Define your non-negotiables — the values, standards, and outcomes that don't bend. Create a simple Decision Rights Matrix outlining who decides what, so no one's guessing where their authority starts or ends. And remember: if productivity only happens when you're watching, you don't have a performance issue, you have a trust issue.

Bonus Check: Revisit your "presence" policies. If your rule is "we need to see you to trust you," you've confused activity with impact.

>>> Give people purpose, not proximity.

2. Coach the *Why*, Not Just the *What*

When someone misfires, don't tighten the leash. Get curious.

Ask: "Walk me through your thinking — what were you solving for?"

Patterns of poor decisions often reveal process gaps, not people gaps.

3. Triage Your Oversight

Not every task deserves your full attention.

- High stakes + low experience → stay close (guide, don't grab).
- Low stakes + high capability → back off.
- Middle ground → set checkpoints, not checkpoints-on-checkpoints.

>>> *You're not removing oversight; you're allocating it intentionally.*

4. Reward Recovery, Not Just Perfection

If your team fears mistakes, they'll play it safe — or hide the truth.

Celebrate people who course-correct fast and share what they learned.

Ownership grows in the space between freedom and forgiveness.

Cheeky Tip

Empowerment isn't tossing someone the keys and hoping for the best. It's teaching them to drive — then trusting them with the car.

The Ownership Mindset

Empowered people don't wait for permission — they see what's needed and make it happen. You'll know you've built ownership when:

- ▸ People make decisions without chasing approval.
- ▸ Risks get flagged early, with solutions attached.
- ▸ Problems arrive with fixes, not excuses.
- ▸ Pride shows up even when no one's watching.

Example: A customer support rep noticed new users were confused during onboarding. Instead of escalating (again), she recorded a short welcome video. Churn dropped 8%. No directive. Just initiative.

Empowerment in Practice

Define the what, not the how.

A retail district manager gave each store a sales goal but let teams design their own local strategies. The result? Real creativity and performance without the babysitting.

Reward initiative, not obedience.

A design firm launched a "Bold Move" award, recognizing smart risks — win or lose. Creativity exploded.

》》》 *When courage counts, innovation follows.*

Coach more, direct less.

A VP ended every one-on-one with, "What support do you need from me?" instead of "Here's what I need from you." The tone, and results changed instantly.

Cheeky Tip

Empowerment isn't about absence. It's about intentional presence. Stay near enough to guide, far enough to let them lead.

Mini Checklist:
Empowering vs. Micromanaging

Ask yourself:

- [ ] Have I clearly defined success?
- [ ] Do people know their decision boundaries?
- [ ] Do I give feedback for learning, not control?
- [ ] Do I check in intentionally — or constantly?
- [ ] Have I made space for others to lead?

If you answered "no" to more than two, congratulations — you've met your inner control freak. Step away from the Slack thread.

Reflection Section

Where are you holding on too tightly — and why?
Is it about their ability, or your comfort?

Leader Lens

Empowerment isn't chaos. It's clarity, courage, and confidence in motion.
Great leaders don't hand off tasks; they hand off trust.

Notes

Do an "empowerment audit."
List two responsibilities you could delegate this week —
and note what boundaries or supports would make them
successful.

Wrapping It Up

If your team can't make a move without your approval, you're not leading — you're blocking.

Empowerment is the oxygen of innovation and accountability.

Start small: hand off one decision you'd normally keep. Then get out of the way.

Guide when needed. Trust always.

Your Challenge

Release the reins — a little.

Replace control with confidence. Watch your people rise to meet it.

Cheeky Reminder

If your team breathes easier when you're on vacation, that *is* your performance review.

18

COMMUNICATION & TRANSPARENCY

Just Say It

People want to be in the loop. Whether it's good news, bad news, or "we're still figuring it out," open communication keeps cultures healthy and people engaged.

Yet leaders keep fumbling this. Some overthink every word, terrified of saying the wrong thing. Others drown messages in approval layers until all authenticity dies. And then there are those who say nothing at all.

(Spoiler: that's the worst option.)

Sure, some conversations require tact. But most of the time, people don't need perfection — they need honesty. They want to understand what's happening and why. They want to feel part of the story, not like extras in someone else's movie.

Why Communication and Transparency Matter

Honesty beats perfection.

When a company facing layoffs held an all-hands meeting, they skipped the spin and corporate polish. Just facts, empathy, and respect.

>>> People can handle bad news. What they can't handle is silence and speculation.

Cheeky Tip

If your "update" sounds like it was written by Legal and translated by AI, everyone knows — and they're already screenshotting it.

Transparency lowers anxiety.

A CEO addressing merger rumors said, "Here's what we know, here's what we don't, and here's when you'll hear from us again."

>>> The unknown is scarier than the truth. When leaders don't talk, people fill in the blanks with worst-case scenarios.

Clarity drives engagement.

A nonprofit connected an operational change directly to its mission — and resistance turned to motivation overnight.

>>> When people understand the *why,* they'll commit to the *how.*

The Anatomy of Great Communication

Lead with honesty.

When a tech company missed a launch, the VP owned it, explained what went wrong, and laid out next steps.

›› Accountability builds credibility faster than excuses ever will.

Be timely.

A startup CEO sent short weekly updates — even when there wasn't much to say. That consistency built stability and trust.

›› A half-baked truth beats a fully baked rumor.

Say it clearly.

Skip the jargon. "We're doubling down on small-business features" beats "We're pivoting to optimize market alignment."

›› Clarity is kindness — speak like a human, not a headline.

Make it two-way.

A retail chain launched quarterly Q&As where anyone could ask leadership anything — no pre-screened questions, no PR guardrails.

›› If your "open-door policy" only applies to compliments, it's not open — it's ornamental.

When Communication Goes Wrong

Overload kills impact.

One company sent a ten-page email about a policy update. Exactly zero people read to the end.

>>> Say less, mean more.

~~~

Over-polishing kills authenticity.

After a data breach, one company said, "We're sorry. We failed you, and here's how we'll fix it." Their competitor wrote, "We are reviewing protocols." Guess which one people forgave.

~~~

Avoiding tough topics kills trust.

Another firm refused to address budget cuts publicly. The silence bred gossip, resentment, and unnecessary exits.

>>> Pretending everything's fine isn't strategy; it's denial.

Cheeky Tip ⌔

If your communication plan is "hope no one notices," they already did.

Success Stories:
Communication Done Right

✧ **Buffer's Transparency Dashboard:** Publicly shares salaries, revenue, and metrics. Radical openness turned into a recruiting magnet.

⬥ **Microsoft's Cultural Reset:** Satya Nadella's candid town halls shifted Microsoft from competitive to collaborative.

⬥ **The Boutique Agency's Bonus Breakdown:** Leadership walked employees through a new bonus structure live — numbers and all. Understanding replaced Slack threads labeled "WTF?"

Micro-Case Study:
Just Say It

A media startup noticed rumors spreading faster than official updates. Instead of policing gossip, they launched a weekly *"Rumor Rundown."* It was direct, funny, and brutally honest. Gossip flatlined, morale spiked, and the company became known for its transparency.

Turns out, truth travels faster than whispers.

Reflection Section

What's one thing your team wishes leadership would just say out loud?

Leader Lens

Transparency doesn't mean oversharing; it means honest clarity.

If you want trust, say what others won't — and say it sooner than you're comfortable.

Notes

Write down one message you've been sitting on.
Now outline how you'll deliver it — clearly,
compassionately, and on time.

Wrapping It Up

Communication and transparency aren't PR tactics — they're leadership in action.

They quiet the noise and help people pull in the same direction. When you hold information hostage, you hold your people hostage too.

Look at your current communication habits. Are they rooted in fear or in trust? In polish or in purpose?

If your updates sound like spin, rewrite them with humanity.

Because great communication isn't about perfect wording — it's about the courage to speak plainly.

Cheeky Reminder

If your employees learn major company news from LinkedIn before hearing it from you, that's not transparency — it's a trust failure.
Fix it before the internet does it for you.

(19)

CHANGE MANAGEMENT

Steering the Ship Through Rough Waters

Change is inevitable.

New tech, new org charts, new "strategic pivots" that sound suspiciously like the last pivot — it never stops.

But here's the thing: not everyone experiences change the same way. Some see opportunity; others see an existential crisis wrapped in a memo.

The secret to leading change isn't pretending everyone will love it. It's showing understanding and providing direction people can trust. Done right, change doesn't just disrupt — it transforms.

Why Change Management Matters

Face emotions, don't ignore them.

When one company moved to remote work, leadership

invited employees into the planning process. They voiced concerns, shaped decisions, and became advocates instead of skeptics.

>>> *People don't fight change — they fight being excluded from it.*

Cheeky Tip

If your plan is "we'll tell them once it's final," don't be shocked when morale drops faster than your email open rates.

Build credibility before you need it.

A manufacturing firm rolling out automation hosted weekly Q&As, answering every question — even the uncomfortable ones.

>>> *People don't follow plans. They follow leaders they believe in.*

Maintain continuity.

When a retail chain shifted to e-commerce, it kept teams grounded by sharing timelines, offering training, and acknowledging fear.

>>> *Change without stability feels like chaos. Change with support feels like progress.*

How to Manage Change Like a Pro

Communicate early and often.

A tech company launching new software shared biweekly updates — wins, misses, next steps. Transparency beat perfection.

>>> *When people know what's happening, they stop guessing.*

Cheeky Tip

"No update" *is* an update.
Say it anyway.

Involve your people.

A hospital invited nurses to pilot new workflows before rollout. Their feedback refined the process, and resistance nearly disappeared.

>>> *Involvement turns "their plan" into "our plan."*

Make it personal.

Skip the corporate speak. Don't say, "This CRM will optimize operations." Say, "This tool saves you two hours of data entry every week."

>>> *Change feels manageable when people see what's in it for them.*

~~~

Support through it — don't just announce it.

When a firm introduced new project-management software, every team got a "change buddy." Training, humor, and consistent check-ins replaced panic.

≫ *Tools don't change behavior — people do.*

> ## *Cheeky Tip* ↶
>
> **Change management without training is just wishful thinking in a nicer font.**

Celebrate progress.

A nonprofit toasted its first campaign run on a new platform. It wasn't perfect, but it was progress.

≫ *Momentum needs fuel. Recognition keeps the sails full.*

When Change Management Goes Wrong

Surprises kill trust.

A company announced layoffs via mass email. The fallout made national headlines.

≫ *People can handle hard news — not ambushes.*

~~~

Ignoring emotion amplifies it.

A retailer shutting stores skipped acknowledging fear. The rumor mill filled the silence.

≫ *Unspoken feelings become friction. Empathy is your cheapest insurance policy.*

Copy-paste strategies backfire.

A global rollout used identical approaches across vastly different regions. Confusion followed.

>>> *Context matters. Tailor your message to the audience, not the org chart.*

Cheeky Tip

"We sent the email" isn't the same as "they understood it."

Success Stories:
Change Done Right

⬦ **Netflix:** Pivoted from DVDs to streaming by communicating a clear vision and re-skilling employees. Disruption turned into dominance.

⬦ **LEGO:** Rebuilt trust during near-bankruptcy by involving employees in redesigning the business. Transparency saved the brick.

⬦ **The Neighborhood Bakery:** Shared behind-the-scenes updates while moving online. Customers felt part of the story — and orders doubled.

Micro-Case Study:
Steering with Empathy

During a chaotic merger, one VP hosted weekly office hours, answered every question honestly, and followed up personally.

Employees didn't love the merger, but they stayed, because they believed her.

Reflection Section

How do you personally respond to change?
What helps you stay grounded when everything around you is shifting?

Leader Lens

Change is inevitable. Chaos is optional.
Great leaders steady the ship by acknowledging fear, communicating clearly, and modeling adaptability.

Notes

Write a "change mantra" you could share with your team — something simple that steadies people when things shift. *(Example: "We'll navigate this together, not alone.")*

Wrapping It Up

Change isn't the villain — resistance and poor communication are.

The best leaders don't eliminate uncertainty; they help people move through it with confidence and calm.

So here's your challenge: Look at your next big shift — a system, a structure, a strategy. Are you *leading* it or merely announcing it?

Because if you're just dropping news and ducking out, that's not leadership — that's an email.

Change doesn't require perfection. It requires direction, empathy, and a steady hand on the wheel.

Cheeky Reminder

If your change plan starts with "We'll figure it out as we go," congratulations — you're already the change that needs managing. Lead better.

20

BUILDING A LEARNING CULTURE

More Than Just Box-Ticking

Call it what you want, but an LMS full of autoplay compliance videos isn't a learning culture — it's background noise.

Real learning isn't about checking boxes. It's about staying curious and wanting to grow — not because you have to, but because it matters to you.

A true learning culture is contagious. It turns mistakes into lessons, experiments into progress, and employees into problem-solvers instead of policy followers.

Why Learning Matters

Curiosity fuels innovation.

A tech company launched an internal "Innovation Lab," inviting employees to pitch and test product ideas. Within six months, one prototype became a top-selling feature.

>>> *When people are encouraged to explore, they stop waiting for permission and start inventing the future.*

Cheeky Tip

If your "innovation strategy" still requires a committee meeting, you're not innovating — you're scheduling.

Learning builds resilience.

During the pandemic, a retail chain trained store managers in digital marketing so they could pivot to e-commerce. Those same managers later led new revenue streams.

>>> *Change favors the curious. The more your people learn, the faster your company adapts.*

Growth inspires engagement.

A healthcare system created a mentorship network pairing senior clinicians with early-career staff. Retention and morale climbed — and so did laughter in the break room.

>>> *People don't quit jobs that invest in them.*

How to Build a Real Learning Culture

Make learning effortless.

A company gave employees one hour a week for self-development and access to LinkedIn Learning — no approvals, no guilt.

>>> *Time isn't the problem; friction is. The easier it is to learn, the more likely people actually will.*

Leaders go first.

A CEO posted monthly "What I Learned This Month" reflections — from leadership podcasts to failed experiments.

>>> *Curiosity at the top legitimizes curiosity everywhere else.*

Cheeky Tip

If your exec team thinks they've mastered leadership, start them on *Humility 101.*

Celebrate learning, not just performance.

At a finance firm's "Spotlight Fridays," anyone could share something new — a skill, an insight, even a mistake.

>>> *When learning is visible, it becomes valuable.*

Make it social.

A nonprofit turned its dull Lunch & Learns into peer-led sessions where employees taught each other everything from Excel hacks to composting.

>>> *When learning feels like connection, not instruction, people show up — and remember it.*

Build learning into the workflow.

A SaaS company introduced "Reflection Wednesdays" — short team sessions to unpack what worked, what didn't, and what they'd try next.

>>> *Learning shouldn't interrupt work; it is the work.*

Cheeky Tip ↰

If people must choose between doing their job and learning, you've designed the wrong job.

When Learning Misses the Mark

One-size-fits-none.

Requiring your engineers to sit through "Sales 101"? Congratulations — you've just invented collective eye-rolling.

>>> *Relevance drives retention.*

~~~

Punitive learning kills curiosity.

Assigning training only after mistakes teaches people to hide problems, not solve them.

>>> *Learning should feel like a privilege, not detention.*

~~~

Ignoring feedback about learning = meta-failure.

HR launches a shiny new platform but ignores login complaints. Within a month, usage tanks.

>>> *A learning culture that doesn't learn is performance art.*

Learning in Action

✧ **Microsoft's Growth Mindset:** Satya Nadella shifted Microsoft from "know-it-all" to "learn-it-all," reigniting innovation and humility.

- **A Start-Up's Learning Fund:** Every employee got $1,000 for personal development — no approvals. Loyalty soared (and so did sushi-class attendance).
- **The Restaurant Chain That Cares:** A fast-food brand trained every level of staff in leadership. Turnover fell 30%, morale doubled. Fries and futures — both done right.

Micro-Case Study:
Learning That Stuck

A mid-sized software company killed its dreaded "training days" and replaced them with *Peer Learning Pods.*

Teams picked their own topics and rotated as teachers — debugging one week, storytelling the next. Participation jumped 80%.

As one developer said, *"It felt less like school and more like growing together."*

That's the point: make learning human, and it sticks.

Reflection Section

What's the most valuable thing you've learned at work this year?

Did it come from a course — or from a real conversation, mistake, or mentor?

Leader Lens

Learning cultures aren't built through platforms; they're modeled through people.

Curiosity, vulnerability, and repetition — that's the formula. Learn out loud.

Notes

Write down one thing you could teach your team this month — and one thing you want to learn from them.

Wrapping It Up

A learning culture isn't about training — it's about transformation.

It's the heartbeat of organizations that refuse to coast.

So here's your challenge: Audit your "learning" today.

Are you inspiring curiosity or assigning homework?

If it's the latter, burn the playbook and start with a question: *What do we actually want people to grow into?*

Because learning isn't just how organizations get smarter — it's how humans become better.

Cheeky Reminder

If your proudest L&D metric is "98% completion," you're not building capability — you're building clickers. Stop counting slides. Start building curiosity.

21

SYSTEMS THAT SCALE HUMANITY

Building What Lasts

B e real — "systems" aren't exactly the stuff of excitement.
    Say the word in a meeting and watch shoulders tighten. People picture endless paperwork and reports that could double as sleep aids.

The reality is that great systems don't choke out humanity — they make it easier to show up fully. They free people from chaos so they can focus on what matters, turning good intentions into real, repeatable action.

And when designed well, they make kindness, clarity, and connection the default setting — not the exception.

Because culture doesn't collapse when people stop caring.

It collapses when the *systems* around them make caring too hard.

Why Systems Matter
(and Why Most Suck)

Systems should create consistency — not kill common sense.

An expense policy requiring five signatures for a $20 lunch doesn't protect resources; it wastes them.

When rules overshadow reason, people stop using judgment — and that's when innovation flatlines.

Processes should reduce friction, not relationships.

A company replaced half its onboarding calls with automated videos. Efficiency? Sure. Connection? Gone.

New hires felt like they'd joined a YouTube playlist, not a team.

System ≠ sameness.

A global retailer let each region personalize its recognition program — handwritten notes in Tokyo, team lunches in Texas.

Same framework, local flavor. Flexibility made the system feel human.

Cheeky Tip

If your "people process" requires three portals, two logins, and a prayer, the problem isn't your people — it's your system.

Building Systems That Serve People

1. Start with the human problem, not the workflow chart.

Ask: What behavior or experience are we trying to enable?

Before redesigning performance reviews, one company asked employees what made feedback meaningful.

The result? A process that felt like coaching, not grading.

When systems begin with empathy, compliance takes care of itself.

2. Design for clarity before layering in tools.

Tech is not a strategy — it's a delivery method.

A startup rolled out a project management tool *after* defining who owned what and why. Adoption skyrocketed because purpose came before platform.

3. Bake humanity into the process.

Embed recognition, feedback, and reflection into the flow of work.

A banking team added one question to every project debrief: *Who deserves a thank-you?*

Morale rose — no extra meetings required.

Human moments don't slow things down; they make things stick.

4. Simplify, ruthlessly.

Complexity is the enemy of execution.

An HR team cut its policy manual from 97 pages to 15 with one rule:

"If we can't explain it in one paragraph, we don't understand it."

People don't follow what they can't remember.

The Sweet Spot:
Structure + Spirit

Systems shouldn't just keep you organized; they should amplify what makes your organization human.

- ▶ Structure without spirit becomes bureaucracy.
- ▶ Spirit without structure becomes chaos.
- ▶ Together? That's scalability.

A nonprofit introduced quarterly *Impact Circles* — structured sessions to review metrics, followed by storytelling about community wins.

Same data, different energy. People left inspired, not inspected.

When systems remind people *why* their work matters, they bring both head and heart to it.

When Systems Go Off the Rails

Death by Data.

A team tracked 47 metrics but could explain maybe five.

They scrapped the excess, focused on what mattered, and suddenly progress felt measurable again.

Policy Paralysis.

An employee spotted a client issue but waited for three approvals before fixing it.

By the time it reached leadership, the client was gone.

Culture as Collateral Damage.

A rigid return-to-office policy ignored flexibility and context.

It didn't rebuild culture — it exposed who never understood it.

> ## Cheeky Tip
> If your system makes good people feel bad for using common sense, it's time for a system update.

Success Stories:
Systems That Scale Humanity

- ◇ **REI:** Their "Opt Outside" policy wasn't a marketing stunt — it became operational DNA. Stores close every Black Friday, employees get paid to go outdoors. The system reinforced values and modeled boundaries. Efficiency stayed high; loyalty skyrocketed.
- ◇ **Zappos:** Their customer-service framework gives reps freedom within guardrails — structured empowerment that lets empathy drive decisions.
- ◇ **A Small Business Win:** A local architecture firm built a shared project playbook with a section called "How We Work Together." Deadlines stayed. Dignity did, too.

Micro-Case Study:
Process with a Pulse

A tech company overhauled quarterly planning, replacing spreadsheets with collaborative workshops.

Each session ended with two prompts: *What excites you?*

What worries you?

Productivity climbed — but so did connection.

Turns out, when people feel part of the plan, they don't just execute it — they own it.

Reflection Section

What's one system in your organization that feels more like a barrier than a bridge?

What would it look like if it prioritized people over process?

Leader Lens

Scalable systems don't replace humanity — they preserve it.

Design structures that make empathy operational and consistency human.

Notes

List two systems you could simplify or humanize this quarter — and who you'd involve in redesigning them.

Notes

Wrapping It Up

The best systems are invisible.

They run quietly in the background so people can shine in the foreground.

They don't steal the spotlight; they make sure it's pointed at the right things.

Take a closer look at your systems — with the same care and curiosity you bring to your culture.

Ask: *Does this process make us more human — or less?*

If it's the latter, scrap it or rewire it. Because the future isn't built on more forms — it's built on better flow.

Cheeky Reminder

If your systems scale process but not people, you're not building a legacy — you're building a machine.
And no one stays loyal to a machine.

CONCLUSION
Small Shifts, Big Impact

Congratulations — you made it to the end of *The Anti-Guide.*
No fluff. No jargon. No "10-step framework to synergy."

Just the truth: meaningful change doesn't start with a grand initiative.

It starts with intention.

The real transformation isn't hiding in a six-figure strategy deck or the latest software subscription.

It lives in the small, human choices leaders make every day — how they communicate, how they show up, how they make people feel.

Because when you shift the small things, the big things start to move on their own.

The Ripple Effect of Small Shifts

The "Good Morning" Revolution
One leader started greeting every team member by name each morning.

That simple, consistent act of presence built belonging faster than any engagement platform ever could.

Multiply that by a hundred leaders and you've got a movement, not a mandate.

Feedback That Fuels, Not Frightens
A single honest, kind, and clear conversation can change the trajectory of someone's growth.

Silence never does.

Caring Costs Nothing (and Pays Ridiculously Well)
Checking in. Remembering. Following through.

It's not hard — it's just rare. And that rarity makes it powerful.

Cheeky Insight
The magic isn't in grand gestures. It's in the daily proof that people matter more than policy memos.

Transformation, Simplified

Forget transformation projects.
Think intentional evolution.

1. Put People First — On Purpose.

Every decision, policy, or "initiative" should pass one test: *What does this actually accomplish for the people doing the work?*

If you can't answer that, you don't have a strategy — you have a slogan.

2. Communicate Like a Human.

People don't need perfect words; they need honest ones.

Over-explaining beats under-communicating every time — but plain language always wins.

Word salads only make everyone hungry and confused.

3. Engagement Isn't Entertainment.

You don't fix culture with pizza parties or hashtag campaigns.

You fix it by building trust, listening deeply, and removing the friction that wears people down.

Fun helps. Belonging sustains.

4. Policies Aren't Progress.

Rolling out a policy without understanding its impact isn't leadership — it's laziness dressed as structure.

Intention is the difference between "checking a box" and actually changing behavior.

If your culture plan has more hashtags than measurable outcomes, you're not transforming — you're marketing.

What Success Actually Looks Like

It's not glossy posters or award plaques.
It's not a "Top Workplace" badge on your website.

It's this:

⟡ People who show up because they *want* to, not because they *have* to.
⟡ Teams that debate openly and celebrate often.
⟡ Leaders who say, "I don't know — let's figure it out together."
⟡ Policies that serve people, not the other way around.

Cheeky Insight

If your version of success is "everyone stays quiet and hits their metrics," congratulations — you've built compliance, not commitment.

Wrapping It Up
(For Real This Time)

Transformation doesn't need a bulldozer; it needs a magnifying glass.

Pay attention to the small moments — the tone of your emails,
the pause before you respond,
the way you close a meeting after asking, "Any questions?"

Those are the moments where culture is built,
trust is earned,
and loyalty quietly takes root.

✦ *Your Final Challenge* ✦

You didn't need a new playbook; you needed permission to toss the old one. That's what this Anti-Guide was always about.

Be intentional.

You don't need another policy to prove control, an event to prove culture, or a memo to prove you're listening.

Mean it, or skip it.

Do everything on purpose.

Lead with clarity.

Communicate with honesty.

Care with intention.

Do that, and you'll build something that outlasts any strategy deck — a culture that feels good to work in and impossible to leave.

If you're still hunting for the magic bullet to fix your organization, here it is:

Give a crap — intentionally.

About your people.

About your culture.

About the ripple effects of every decision you make.

That's it. That's the whole playbook.

Now go lead like you mean it.

www.ingramcontent.com/pod-product-compliance
Lightning Source LLC
Chambersburg PA
CBHW040923210326
41597CB00030B/5158